Praise for *When Calling Parents Isn't Your Calling*

Why read *When Calling Parents Isn't Your Calling: A teacher's guide to communicating with all parents*? Because when you are talking with parents, you are stepping on dreams – you need to step-lightly! Crystal Frommert provides valuable guidance whether you are new to the parent communications responsibility of teaching or experienced and dealing with the continuously changing school issues or the changing forms of communication. She illustrates specific examples of challenging messages with concrete strategies to consider. You can use this resource to consciously plan a message as well as to reflect on messages you have sent that did or did not connect as you wanted them to. Communicate your competence, confidence, and professionalism.

Steve Barkley
Executive VP and Chief Learning Officer,
PLS 3rd Learning

In her practical, wise new guide to parent-teacher communication, Crystal Frommert brings decades of experience in schools to bear on all the problems that can arise in that fraught relationship. She covers it all: back-to-school night, when the teacher has made a mistake, and why those exhausting classroom newsletters will never substitute for direct communication. Beginning teachers will find Ms. Frommert's guide extremely useful; veteran teachers will find it an affirming trip down a battle-scarred road.

Michael Thompson
Co–author of Hopes and Fears: Working with
Today's Independent School Parents

Crystal Frommert's experience in the classroom shines through in her practical tips that can improve communication and collaboration with parents.

Robert Evans, Ed.D.
Co-author of Hopes and Fears: Working with
Today's Independent School Parents

As educators, we may receive professional development in topics such as classroom management, student engagement, and grade specific curriculum. Unfortunately, one area educators are generally not prepared for is how to effectively communicate with parents. This critical skill is often barely touched upon in teacher preparation programs. Crystal Frommert addresses this need in her book, *When Calling Parents Isn't Your Calling: A teacher's guide to communicating with parents*. This book provides helpful strategies to effectively communicate with families, ease anxiety over connecting with parents, strengthen parent-teacher relations, and so much more. This is a fantastic read with many great takeaways for educators of all experience levels.

Brian Martin
Second Grade Teacher, Speaker,
Host of the Teaching Champions Podcast

Crystal Frommert shares poignant stories of her own and other educators' successes and failures in building partnerships with parents and other significant grownups through effective communication. Her engaging narrative spans the traditional in-person parent–teacher conference to the opportunities and pitfalls afforded by phone calls, newsletters, emails, text messages and the newer forms of social media. With the social political ethos of our time, she describes how implicit biases interfere with communicating respectfully with adults holding strong and nuanced opinions on matters of racial inequity and gender identification. Her insightful reflections and thoughtful suggestions will serve both the novice and experienced teacher well.

Robert McPherson
Former Dean of Education University of Houston

Crystal is a fantastic writer and always ahead of the curve when it comes to what's happening in schools. She writes engaging, conversational content that is completely relatable. Working with her has been a joy as her ideas are always on target and impactful! Overall, I highly recommend her book!

Heather Cherry
Content Manager
Independent School Management

Crystal Frommert has constructed a great mix of principles, advice, and classroom stories to help develop better communication between parents and teachers. As a teacher educator, I'm painfully aware that there's little we can do to prepare novice teachers for this. So I'm very happy to have this accessible, practice-based resource to share with them.

John Golden
Professor of Mathematics
Grand Valley State University

WHEN
CALLING
PARENTS
—*isn't*—
YOUR
CALLING

A teacher's guide
to communicating
with parents

Max's Dad

BY CRYSTAL FROMMERT

When Calling Parents Isn't Your Calling:
A teacher's guide to communicating
with parents

Cover design and artwork by
Greg Frommert

Road to Awesome, LLC.

To Kate and Greg.
You are my everything.

Table of Contents

Introduction   1

Chapter 1 – Why connect with parents?   7

Chapter 2 – But I have a class newsletter;   21
isn't that enough?

Chapter 3 – Why is parent communication   33
so hard?

Chapter 4 – Reach out effectively.   41

Chapter 5 – What about the difficult 10%?   55

Chapter 6 – What if I am wrong?   81

Chapter 7 – Have the hard conversations.   99

Chapter 8 – How to communicate with parents with   111
varying levels of engagement

Chapter 9 – Parent-teacher conferences and   137
parent night

Chapter 10 – Report card comments and narratives   151

Conclusion   159

Acknowledgements   165

References   167

About the Author   179

Introduction

As a new teacher in 2000, I was, to be frank, terrified of interacting with parents. Essentially, all parent contact was through signed papers, phone calls, and face-to-face meetings. Back then, I had one parent with an email address, and I remember thinking to myself, "What am I going to do with an email address?" Of course, email existed in 2000 but not as a common method for a teacher to communicate with parents. My undergrad years in the college of education and student teaching did basically nothing to prepare me for parent communication. Because of my inexperience and fear, partnering with parents seemed like an unattainable goal.

Fast forward to my 20th year of teaching, and I feel much more at ease partnering with parents. This comes from experiences that were successful and some that were failures. When I began writing for the online educational publication Edutopia, my first piece focused on building relationships with parents. I chose this as my first topic because of my own professional growth in this area and the struggles my colleagues and I were having with parent communication. I worked with teacher colleagues who really hated making phone calls, didn't reply to emails for days (or ever), or didn't see the value in a parent partnership. The Edutopia article sparked so many conversations online and in real life that I felt inspired to share my journey through parent partnerships in a book for educators. This book will give educators in all stages of their careers in all grade levels practical tips and language to improve communication with parents and get the conversations started.

Some of the strategies and tips laid out in this book may not apply to all communities or situations. I do address boundaries and exceptions in the chapters. Assess the situation and go with your gut on what decisions to make - it is absolutely key that we listen to our intuitions when they speak to us.

A note about nomenclature: the word *parents* is used throughout the book. As educators, we know that not all students live with their parents. Some families consist of aunts/uncles, grand-parents, siblings, or foster families raising our students. It is important to take the extra effort to learn the family dynamic so that you are using the correct labels and names when talking about a student's family. In a September 2020 Parents Magazine article, author and former teacher Glennon Doyle suggests, "Please consider saying 'your grownups.' I used that when I was teaching and it helped. Adults' language can determine children's belonging."

When I don't know much about the families of the students I am talking to, I use the word grown-ups. For simplicity purposes, this book will use the word *parent(s)* to mean an adult or the adults who are caregivers for your students.

This book can be read alone or as a book study. Keep a copy on your desk for quick reference if you find yourself in a parent communication dilemma. The questions that are included at the end of each chapter are there to guide you in reflecting on your own experiences or to spark group discussions.

An ironic situation occurred while writing this introduction. I was given constructive feedback by my supervisor regarding my parent communication. My supervisor, the head of school, shared a parent complaint about my tone in an email. The entire time he was informing me about the parent complaint I was thinking, "I am writing a book on effective parent communication. How can I be getting negative feedback on this? I am supposed to be good at this!" I thanked him for his feedback and offered my perspective on the incident. Apparently, this particular parent did not appreciate that I quickly shot off an email to her about a reminder to complete a required school form. I wrote it so hastily that the message lacked polite language. To add to my faux pas, I even missed a typo in my curt message. To be completely honest, I was irritated that the form was not yet complete, and I typed the email while frustrated and hurried. Little did I know that my hastily-sent email would result in a conversation in the head's office. All's well that ends well, and now, I am more aware of how my communication comes across when I am hurried and frustrated. I was embarrassed, yes, but more aware, nonetheless.

I added this story to the introduction to show that no matter how many years of experience an educator has or how successful they have historically been with parent relationships, mistakes will happen. We will have bad days. We will make poor judgment calls. There will also be times that we do everything exactly right and still make a parent upset. We have to pick ourselves up and keep trying. We have to keep trying for the sake of our students. It would be easy to write off this complaining parent and be forever annoyed, but because I value their child's education and well-being, I have to do whatever I can to make it right and build the bridge.

Chapter 1
Why connect with parents?

As a middle school educator and administrator, I have attended several overnight trips with my students, primarily to Washington DC or local camps. These trips serve as an educational experience - learning about history or nature, depending on the location. The most important purpose, however, is building class unity and independence in our middle schoolers. (Parent chaperones do not attend the trips for this reason.) I recall one particular trip to Washington DC in which the teacher chaperones texted the parents of the students in the group with updates and photos. The parents loved it. Some would even text back with helicopter-type requests, "Can you please tell Aiden to wear his raincoat tomorrow?" This was the first trip I had chaperoned with that level of parent communication. The students were even allowed to have their cell phones for a designated amount of time each day to call their parents. To be honest, I thought this was overkill. "Calm down, and let your kids enjoy their trip without their parents!"

I would say inside my head with an internal eye roll.

Ironically, exactly 24 hours after I returned home, my own middle school child left for her school's camping trip. The rules for this trip were more traditional than the school where I worked. No student cell phones allowed. No expectation of chaperone group texts to parents. There was a trip blog that was inconsistently updated with general information. There was no way for me to remind my daughter to wear her raincoat. No way to communicate at all. My annoyance took a 180 degree turn from the trip I had chaperoned the week before. I wanted photos, I wanted updates, I desperately wanted to know that my child was happy, warm, dry, and safe. It's remarkable how my perspective flip-flopped within a day between the two trips. It's perfectly understandable – it's my kid we're talking about here! Whether you are an educator who is a parent or not, it is important that we consider both perspectives. Yes, we want students learning independence and agency. While at the same time, their parents are worried night and day about their most precious treasures. There is a balance to be struck, and it is not always easy.

You probably didn't pick up this book because working with parents is your favorite part of your job. Your heart might light up at the sight of snaggletooth smiles and the sound of happy laughter on the playground. Or maybe you work with older kids, and you are filled with joy when a kid overcomes a challenge in class or writes you a thank you note for helping them learn. None of these scenarios involve a parent email or conference.

Years ago, I remember sitting uncomfortably in a preschooler-sized chair at my daughter's Meet the Teacher night. Her teacher started off her presentation with, "If I seem nervous it's because I am used to talking to much shorter people." It got a chuckle from the room full of parents who were probably equally as nervous to be parents of preschoolers. The teacher was spot-on with that comment. Most educators entered the teaching profession to work with young people – talking to adults is not our preferred way to spend the day.

If you have been teaching for decades, it might appear to others that you have an ease about you when talking with parents. Early in my career, I remember admiring experienced teachers who greeted parents as if they were old friends. Who knows, maybe they were old friends? However, even the most seasoned veteran can get rattled by an angry parent. But whether we like it or not, we have to meet with parents as part of our job to educate kids, even the parents who are pushy, irate, anxious, and exceedingly loquacious. We need to learn to value parent interactions, approach tough conversations with confidence and empathy, and maybe even get so comfortable that we greet parents like old friends.

I have been blessed throughout my 20 plus year career to work with many amazing professionals who have modeled healthy parent relationships. Many of the stories and suggestions in the following chapters come from colleagues who have offered me guidance. I have made many missteps in my career as well that have shaped me as an educator and administrator. I inserted these stories to help others learn from my mistakes too.

WHY DO WE NEED TO VALUE PARENT INTERACTIONS?

I worked with a young, no-nonsense principal early in my career who was wise well beyond his years. As the school leader of a public junior high with 1900 students in a building that only comfortably held 1500, he had to work some sort of magic to keep the school running smoothly. He once said to the faculty, "These parents are sending you the best they have. They're not hiding their good kids at home." I'll admit it was a bizarre thing to say, but his point was that parents were sending their absolute pride and joy to school. He expected his faculty and staff to remember this in every interaction with a parent, even the tough interactions. When talking with parents about their children, it is far more emotional than talking about any other topic. Sayde Campoamor noted in an NPR CodeSwitch interview, consider the brain science behind conversations about people's children, "...when you talk to people in general about their kids, you're talking to their amygdalas. And an amygdala is a part of your brain that's the lizard brain that's like 'threat, threat, threat'." (Freedman, 2022)

A few times, I had to tell parents that their pride and joy was struggling in my math class or that they had misbehaved in class. No matter how they responded to this news, I had to always remember that if we did not work as partners, I could not do my job effectively. I needed that parent to support their child at home, support the work I sent home, and work toward the same goals for their child's success. I needed that parent to trust me as a professional educator and also trust that I made decisions with their child's best interest in mind.

Stories from the Field

Miss A of York, NE

I was called in to sit with a student after his parent died since I lost my mom as a kid.

A year later, on the anniversary of my mother's death, I received a note from the surviving parent. She was checking in on me.

Grief brings people together; it's a shared experience.

One August, a father requested to meet with me a couple of days before school started. They were a new family in our school. I had not yet met his daughter, so I came into the meeting with no background knowledge of her personality, strengths, or abilities. Regardless, I knew that we needed to partner up to have a successful year. He called the meeting to insist that his daughter needed to skip my math course and advance to the next year's math course because of her math aptitude. He came prepared with her work samples and her previous standardized test results. The bottom line was that our school did not allow students to skip math courses in the sixth grade. It was hard to convince the dad of this fact based on precedence alone. I shared with him all of the topics we would explore in this course beyond what she had studied before, such as math history and social justice connections. It was not an easy sell, but we eventually agreed that his daughter would start my class in two days. I assured him that I would watch her progress closely and supplement with more advanced material if I found she had already mastered the content in any unit. He left satisfied that his daughter's new math teacher would look out for her and support her learning, even if it meant customized materials. (Spoiler alert: she was indeed advanced in math, and the supplementary material she received was the same that five other students in the class also received throughout the year. She was definitely in the right math course.)

WORKING WITH PARENTS WITHIN HEALTHY BOUNDARIES

Partnering with parents doesn't mean catering to their demands. Like a good doctor would work with a patient toward a healthy solution, a teacher works with the parent toward a solution that is best for the student. If an overbearing parent wants to walk their middle schooler to the classroom door every day, we have to take a firm stance that this behavior is not best for their child. If a parent expects you to spend a disproportionate amount of your resources on their child, you can set boundaries around what is reasonable. The hard part is convincing the parent to partner with us on this decision.

Try the following sentence stems to get the conversation started.

"The last time we spoke regarding Joey's behavior in class, I appreciated your support in helping him move forward and correct his behavior. I am hoping that we can work together again to resolve this issue."

"I absolutely see your point of view here that _____. Additionally, Samantha needs to develop skills that will help her _____."

"Did Joanna tell you about what happened at lunch yesterday? I am curious what you heard at home."

HAPPY NOTES

Whether you teach little kids or big kids, many parents want to hear happy things from their child's teacher. Early in my career, I was given fantastic advice to make sure your first interaction with a parent is a positive one. If you suspect that you will need to contact the parents of a particular child with a negative message, then reach out very early to get the positive message out when you can. As a math teacher, I took the time to write a personalized email to each family during the first week of school. To save time writing dozens of similar messages, the bulk of the body of the email was copied and pasted. I was sure to add something personal to the email.

> Dear Biel-Timberlake family,
> It is a pleasure to have Jessica in Algebra I this year. She brings enthusiasm and curiosity to the class that inspires others.
> I am looking forward to meeting you at Parent Night on September 16 at 7 pm.
> In the meantime, please check out our class website at…

Writing an email for each family takes a while, but the investment of time that you put in during the early weeks will pay off for the rest of the year. The parents get a good impression of you as the teacher, and they know that you know their child.

As mentioned in a college-level textbook under the Contacting and Communicating with Parents section, Dr. Paul R. Burden (2020) stresses the need for positive communication. He states that constant communication with parents results in more supportive parents when an issue may come up later. Research by Dr. John Gottman (2022) suggests that healthy relationships thrive with a five-to-one ratio of positive to negative interactions.

While his work is mostly referring to marital relationships, perhaps we can extend this ratio to our relationships with parents as well. If you have one negative encounter with a parent, keep hope that you can counter it with five positive ones. This might sound like a lofty goal, but there are small ways to reach your ratio of five-to-one, such as randomly sent happy notes. Sending happy notes to parents throughout the year is one of the most rewarding ways to spend a few minutes of your day. A happy note is a short message telling a parent that their child has done something remarkable. The meaning of remarkable has a broad range here. The best time to send a happy note is when a child, who typically only receives negative notes or calls, has shown improvement or has completed a positive task. The note can be as simple as:

> *Good afternoon Drs. Carrington,*
> *I am sending this short note to let you know*
> *that Blake was one of the few students who*
> *solved the Problem of the Week this week - it*
> *was a challenging one. Blake enthusiastically*

worked out his solution to the problem on
the board for his classmates. I am
impressed with how hard he worked to solve
this problem.
Have a great day!

Without sounding too transactional, sending messages like this are like deposits into the parent partnership bank. Like a bank account, the balance is maintained through deposits and withdrawals. You want to keep a positive balance. Blake's parents may not be as willing to partner with a teacher who only gives negative feedback about his progress.

Sending happy notes doesn't have to take a lot of time. Using a printed roster of your class, make a small dot next to a student's name each time you send such a message. Try to make it through the roster by the end of each grading term or half of the school year. If you're having a crummy day, sending happy notes is almost guaranteed to perk up your mood because often, parents reply with equally happy notes. One parent replied to me, "I was having a really terrible day, but your message made it all better!" I also got lucky once and received this reply, "Today happens to be my birthday, and I could not ask for a better gift than a nice message about Sarah."

Partnering with parents can also head off potential academic and discipline issues. In the 2013 book *No More Taking Away Recess and Other Problematic Discipline Practices* (Sawyer & Cassetta) the authors include a section titled "Talk with and about families." This section advises educators to "talk to families early on about your students." The story told in this section involves a sixth grade girl whose mother was getting remarried to a man the child didn't like. This life event was causing a lot of stress for the student. The teacher was in contact with the child's mother frequently therefore, was able to frame the child's display of being distant and critical in a way that allowed the teacher to support her because he knew the cause of her behavior. The teacher and the parent partnered to support the student to use writing as a way to express her anger in a healthy way. By staying in close communication with the child's family, the teacher was able to redirect the negative behavior which benefited both the home and the classroom environment.

REFLECTION

- If you're a parent, think back to an interaction you have had with your child's teacher. What made the interaction positive? What could have been improved?

- If you're not a parent, ask a family member or close friend about their interactions with their child's teachers.

- If you were to send out an anonymous survey to the parents of the students in your class, predict how they would respond to the question, "How can communication with my child's teacher be improved?"

- Have all of your students' parents heard from you already this school year? What is the ratio of happy notes to negative notes for each student?

- If a student is demonstrating unproductive behavior in the classroom, what efforts have you made to learn more about the child's background and home life?

Chapter 2

But I have a class newsletter; isn't that enough?

As an educator and as a parent I have seen several classroom newsletters that provide insights into the learning that happens at school – I have to admit that most of the time I delete them when they come to my inbox. I am a little ashamed of this, but these newsletters are just too wordy, too impersonal, and sometimes, not very interesting. As blogger/podcaster Jennifer Gonzalez stated in her 2015 article "Why No One Reads Your Classroom Newsletter," include a call to action for parents to take as a result of reading the information. "...here's where the newsletter can be a powerful instrument in the parent-teacher partnership: The next time you write your newsletter, consider what you ideally want parents to do as a direct result of reading it."

Educator Erika Walther, a writer for the Truth for Teachers blog, suggests ways to personalize communication with parents (2022). Just as you would differentiate ways to reach students in your class, you can diversify your communication methods to reach more parents. Walther suggests offering options beyond the traditional newsletter on your website, such as texting, Zoom meetings, and offering flexible meeting times. As reported from a 2021 study by Firefly Learning (Banister, 2021), Dan Locke-Wheaton, principal of Aston University Engineering Academy, said,

> It's hugely encouraging to know parents are positive about their child's school and that so many would like to receive more information about their child's learning. The challenge for schools is how we can provide this without it taking too much time. For me, technology can play a vital role, giving parents – and teachers – the flexibility to engage with parents at a time and place of their choosing.

A clever suggestion from the 2005 book *The Tactful Teacher: Effective Communication with Parents, Colleagues, and Administrators*, by

Yvonne Bender, is having your students create the class newsletter. This idea is probably best suited for upper elementary classes. Parents would definitely read the class newsletter if little Reagan authored the feature article about the recent class field trip.

PERSONALIZE COMMUNICATION BEYOND A NEWSLETTER TO REACH MORE PARENTS

An important point Erika Walther makes in her article (2022) is to assume the best intent from parents. "We cannot write off the children who we have not yet been able to reach. Those are the students who may need us the most, if not as a teacher, then as an advocate." My previous school used to schedule back-to-back, 15-minute, in-person parent conferences that ran on a schedule as tight as a German train timetable. The harsh reality was if a parent was late, too bad. One year, a mom and dad did not arrive for their scheduled appointment. I waited and waited. No phone call, no email. I was already frustrated, but my frustration grew tenfold when I saw them approach my classroom at the end of my long day of dozens of conferences. I greeted them with a tense smile as they apologetically explained that they rescued an injured dog on the way to their appointment. They couldn't call or email because they were dealing with taking the dog to the veterinarian. They were so sorry, but could they please meet now? My frustration melted instantly. From that point on, I never again assumed the worst of a parent who didn't make it on time for a meeting.

Walther also mentioned boundaries and exceptions to those boundaries. Having flexibility in your communication doesn't mean giving out your personal cell number and taking calls and texts through the night and weekend. There are always exceptions, however. If you need to talk to a parent from your cell phone make it clear you are calling from this number because it is urgent. If the parent abuses this exception, you have the right to not respond, and call them from a school phone the next day. On a field trip with eighth graders, I gave my personal cell number to one parent because of her son's unique medical condition. She was extremely grateful for the direct line of communication and never abused this access. I am sure other parents would have also liked for me to text updates and respond to their questions during the trip, but I stuck to my boundary.

As a parent, I remember one of my daughter's teachers writing in her welcome letter that she only checked email at the end of the day because she was teaching children all day, which made a lot of sense. Any message sent in the morning or midday about early pick-up, carpool changes, medications, or any other immediate needs would not be read by her until after school. Parents needed to contact the front desk for these types of messages. It was honest, efficient, and clear.

ONLINE GRADEBOOKS ARE NOT A SUBSTITUTE FOR TEACHER-PARENT COMMUNICATION

As an algebra teacher long before online grades, I would write test grades very small in the top corner of the paper. In larger print, with a brightly-colored marker, I would write the student's current average in my class. This was beneficial to the students in three ways.

1. It forced me to make sure my gradebook was up-to-date with all grades including the current test score.

2. It showed the kids that their overall average may not have suffered as much as they predicted if their test grade was lower than they anticipated. (I wrote the test score very small to emphasize that individual scores are less significant than overall progress.)

3. Because parents were required to sign each test, parents also could see their current progress in the course.

My students and I were cruising along just fine with this process, and then my school decided to move to online grades. In my unpopular opinion, this decision was not a positive change for our parents, students, or faculty for a few reasons. A live gradebook could potentially nurture the grades-obsessed culture amongst some of my students and the helicopter-ness of many parents. I no longer had the motivation to keep my gradebook up to date by the time I returned graded tests to the students. I became complacent in proactively contacting parents about grades or missing work because I figured they were checking their kids' grades online and were aware of their progress. Wrong. Independent School Management published a helpful article in 2019 titled, "Fives Do's and Don'ts of Effective Parent Communication." The first item on the list was, "Don't think that online gradebooks replace progress reports or spontaneous feedback on a child's performance."

COMMUNICATE EARLY

One of the most dreaded but preventable questions an administrator can hear from a parent is "Why didn't I know about this issue with my child before?" As a parent myself, I have to agree that this is something many educators can improve upon when it comes to communicating issues. Supportive parents can't help the situation if they do not know about it. If a student is missing a few assignments in a row, forgetting supplies more often, or suddenly performing poorly in a unit of study, let the parents know. If a student's behavior is disrupting their learning or the other students' learning, talk to the parents about it. They may be able to help solve the problem at home before it escalates.

As mentioned in the 2018 Edutopia article "5 Strategies for a Successful Parent-Teacher Conference," 25-year veteran teacher Emelina Minero advises, "Don't wait for problems to arise. Make it a point to communicate frequently and positively so that you have already developed a relationship before you hit bumps in the road."

I have heard many reasons why teachers don't do this.

"If I contact the parents, they'll blame me and/or defend their child."

Yes, this can happen. *But at least you have documentation that you have communicated the concern to the parent. We cannot control their reaction.*

"I have X amount of students and hardly any prep periods, I do not have the time to contact parents for every little thing."

This is a real problem, no doubt about that. *Talk to your administrator. Let them know that you want to reach out to parents more often, but there is little space for this in your schedule. If this doesn't help, try some time-saving tips such* as creating a template email that is sent to parents for various scenarios. Fill in the child's name and some details and, voilà, you have an email ready to go. It's not very personal, but it gets the job done.

> **"These kids are in X grade, they are old enough to keep track of their own academics/responsibilities."**

Maybe, but as educators, we know kids develop at different rates. So do parents. Not all parents are ready to let their middle or high schoolers take full responsibility for their grades. They have the pressures of applying to colleges, and a low mark on their report card for academics or behavior can have exponentially worse consequences. Invite the parents to partner with you before it comes to that.

ADJUST COMMUNICATION FOR EVENTS

As mentioned in the first chapter, my child's school posted general information on a blog during a week-long camping trip. What I really wanted as a parent was photos and personalized updates. Am I asking for too much from teacher chaperones trying to keep 100 middle schoolers safe and engaged on a camping trip? Yes, most definitely. But, however irrational my desire was, some personalized communication would have eased my anxiety.

Teachers and administrators can anticipate high-anxiety times in the school year where increased parent communication is helpful and stress-reducing. Some of these times might be before the first day of school, parent conferences, field trips, final exams, or upcoming ceremonies like graduation. Sending reminder emails repeating the protocols or itinerary adds extra work for school employees, but it can be incredibly helpful to parents.

Follow up emails are also reassuring. After taking 55 seventh graders on a four-day trip, I took a few hours the day after we returned to send a personalized email to each family. I included a personal anecdote about their child and thanked them for their excellent behavior on the trip. My personalized email shaped the narrative that the trip was a huge success, just in case a child went home to complain about our delayed flight, lack of vegetarian food options at one restaurant, or rainy weather. Those things may have also been true but not what I wanted parents to take away from the overall trip experience.

REFLECTION

- If you have a newsletter, how are you gathering data to see if the information is read by families? Is the information valued by families? How can you get creative with the media you use in your mass communication such as videos or photos?

- Do you differentiate your communication between families? How do you avoid the perception that you might be playing favorites?

- If your school has online gradebooks, how do you communicate progress to supplement this grade reporting system?

- What times of the school year can you anticipate that increased informational communication might be helpful?

Chapter 3

Why is parent communication so hard?

In my early years as a teacher, I nervously started all parent phone calls with, "I am sorry to bother you at work…" A colleague who had many more decades of experience overheard me say this. She pulled me aside afterward to advise me to never say, "sorry to bother you." Her recommendation was to start off the conversation with, "Is this a good time to talk about Juliet's progress?" This initial question gives the parents a chance to move to a private room at work or pull over if they are in the car. Additionally, you're not sorry to call them to talk about their child. You are partnering with the parent for the benefit of their child's progress.

TO CALL OR NOT TO CALL

Nowadays, with email being the most popular and most convenient mode of communication, it is rare that I will cold call a parent. Instead, I set aside a chunk of time a few days per week

33

for parent calls and emails. When setting up a call, email first with, "Are you available today between 3-4 pm or tomorrow from 9-9:30 am to discuss Ralph's recent quiz? What number is best to call?" This type of email is beneficial in three ways.

1. It eliminates wasting time playing phone tag.

2. The parents have a heads up and won't be caught by surprise. No one likes an unsolicited phone call.

3. The phone call will occur at a predetermined time that works for your schedule.

Michael Goldstein, author of *Phoning Parents: High-leverage moves to transform your classroom & restore your sanity* (2013), encourages teachers to dedicate time every evening to calling parents for check-ins, praises, and corrections. Goldstein's idea, based on research, is that calling parents will increase the odds of students completing their work, reduce the amount of time teachers spend redirecting students, and students raise their hands more.

HOW DO WE LEARN TO CONNECT?

We know it's important to connect with parents. If you are a parent yourself, you know what it is like to receive communication from your child's school. But how do educators learn how to communicate effectively? Some college communication or marketing courses directly teach effective methods of delivering a message to clients and the public. Many educators enter the teaching profession through the College of Education route, which is not particularly known for teaching communication skills to other adults. We have classes that go into great, research-based detail on how to teach children how to write and decode words. Do we, as educators in training, learn how to write an email or decode a parent's perspective? One might argue, "How hard is it to write an email or have a tough conversation with a parent?" One might argue back, "This is very hard when your full-time job is teaching 20 kindergartners with little time dedicated to talking to grown-ups." Parent communication is something that must be approached carefully to maintain the necessary relationship needed for student success.

Education majors often end their degrees by interning in a classroom through student-teaching or another similar program that provides experience with teaching and classroom management. Is this the semester we learn effective parent communication? When do pre-service teachers get an opportunity to lead a parent conference or phone call? Even if this opportunity is available, the supervising teacher would give the pre-service teachers the easy parent situations as a practice. During my own student-teaching semester, I did have the opportunity to sit in on a few parent conferences but only as a silent observer. The first difficult parent meetings come during the first year of a teacher's career when they have no direct experience de-escalating parent situations on their own.

If you have a connection to teacher prep organizations, here are some questions you might want to ask:

- Could we offer mock parent conferences for practice and assessment? Would it be beneficial to have admin/coaches/counselors sit in on first-year teacher meetings? Would this undermine the teacher?

(Maybe this is happening in some Colleges of Education.)

- Can student-teachers contribute to parent-teacher conferences, even the difficult conversations?

- What required course curriculum exists for helping pre-service teachers learn effective parent communication?

If you know of a pre-service teacher or a new teacher, pass this book on to them. Also, know that walking the tightrope of parent relationships takes years of trial and error, and even then it will not be flawless. These are some habits you can adopt to actively increase your effectiveness with parent communication no matter how long you've been teaching:

- If you notice a colleague who has the gift of wordsmithing or email crafting, save their emails, maybe to a personal account so that you can reference them even if you change schools later. Jot down notes as they speak to build a collection of phrases you want to use later.

- Read parenting books for the age level you teach. You might not regularly give parenting advice, but understanding what parents are going through at home will add empathy to your communication.

- If you have a colleague who is also a parent of a student similar in age to the students you teach, ask them to proofread your emails or report card comments to get their perspective.

- Ask a mentor or instructional coach on your campus to role-play a parent conference with you. (I did this as an instructional coach. It was fun playing the role of a frustrated and slightly bitter mom.)

No matter where you are in your career or what your teacher training was like, you always have opportunities to grow and learn. Each time you make a mistake with parent communication (which will happen from time to time), treat each hiccup as a learning opportunity for the future.

REFLECTION

- What were the most difficult parent interactions you have had? How did they end up? Was there anything you could have done differently?

- Were there times you wished you had called rather than sent an email? Were there times you wish you had sent an email rather than called?

- What advice would you give to a new teacher wanting to learn more about parent communication?

- If you had someone role-play a parent conference with you, in what scenario would you need the most help? What is your biggest fear that you know you need practice facing?

- Think back to your pre-service teaching training (this might be current for some readers and decades ago for others). What practice did you get communicating with parents? Did you have a strong role model for parent communication?

Chapter 4

Reach out effectively.

One of the best advice nuggets I have ever learned from a colleague happened during a middle school team meeting with a parent. The child was struggling in a few classes and the parent requested that each of the teachers email them every time their child had a missing assignment. This would be tough a commitment to make with all of the demands a teacher encounters in a day. One genius teacher in the room suggested that the parents email the team of teachers weekly asking for an update and that we would be glad to reply with a summary of the child's progress for the week. She emphasized that this was a temporary solution to help the child get back on track. The beauty of a once-a-week progress check was that it gave the child and teacher some space from the constant hovering of the parents. Additionally, placing the onus on the parent relieves the teacher of the pressure to remember to email for one particular child out of dozens. As a middle school administrator, I suggested this option to parents when their child was struggling academically or organizationally. I would send this message to the grade level team and the parents: "As we discussed in our meeting today, Mr. and Mrs. Redenbacher will be emailing the team once per week to check in on Orville's progress." This follow-up email confirms that the parents are responsible for the next step and also gives the teachers a heads up. In my experience, the weekly emails usually stop after only two or three weeks.

EMAIL: FRIEND OR FOE?

I used to be an *inbox zero* type of teacher, meaning I aimed to clear out my inbox by tackling every message that was sent to me. As an administrator, that goal was way back in my rearview mirror. Inboxes are like the game of Whack-a-Mole; you conquer one message and two more pop up. It's a never-ending battle. I realized I had a problem when I received this email from a parent, "I have a question about my child's physics class. I know you do not teach physics, but you're so fast to reply to emails so maybe you can help me get in touch with the physics teacher?" By being efficient with email, I inadvertently created a reputation for myself that resulted in more busy work. Now, I use the email's snooze and send later features (available on Gmail and Outlook). When I get an email I know I want to respond to eventually, I snooze it for another time or day. If I want to compose a reply immediately but also don't want to get the reputation of a quick responder, I use the send later feature.

Gina of Arlington, TX

Our school has computer monitoring software that alerts the teachers if a student is searching for questionable content. I received an alert that a 5th grader searched the word, "sex." Worried about what search results might come up, I sent a friendly heads-up email to his mom. The next day at carpool, she told me how grateful she was that I emailed her. She added with a laugh that she took a screenshot of my email and texted it out to her extended family with the message, "Happy Hump Day!" Her family sounds fun, I just hope the kid wasn't too embarrassed.

Use email only for short but thoughtful messages. If the topic is sensitive or hard to describe in writing, send an email asking for a phone call. Offer up times that are convenient for you and let the parent pick from the times you offered. It is kind to offer some hint at why you're asking for a phone call such as, "Do you have some time today to discuss Jake's recent quiz?" This gives parents a heads up so they're not thinking the worst. Michael Goldstein offers a smart recommendation in his book, *Phoning Parents* (2013). He suggests starting a phone conversation with a time check. Goldstein stresses that parent phone calls should take 2-5 minutes and starts with a statement like, "I need 5 minutes of your time to talk about Nash. Is this a good time for you?" In my experience, parents would more often than not take up more than 2-5 minutes with follow-up questions, sharing their woes, and *while I have you on the phone* irrelevant topics. To be fair, if I called parents on a regular schedule, as Goldstein recommends, they would be familiar with my two-minute check-in phone calls. Consider how check-in calls would resonate with your parent population. I suspect most parents today would not pick up the phone if it rang from an unknown number.

I worked with an old school principal who half-jokingly suggested that we eliminate all parent to teacher emails. He suggested that communication should be only by phone or notes. He knew that this wasn't possible, but he did make an excellent point. Email can get messy and confusing. For younger students, a daily notebook might be an alternative to emails. The teacher writes a short message only when needed in the notebook, and parents can do the same. My own child's daily notebook in pre-kindergarten once came home with a note about how she was struggling to share with her classmates. The note was accompanied by a children's picture book about sharing. When a teacher's note is accompanied by a book, you know the teacher is sending a strong message.

CULTURE AROUND ELECTRONIC COMMUNICATION

Each school has a different culture around parent communication. In my experience, many schools have a 24-hour reply rule for parent emails - even if your reply is simply, "Thank you for reaching out. I will look into this and get back to you soon." You want to respond to every parent's email either with a reply or a phone call. Author of *Digital Body Language: How to Build Trust and Connection, No Matter the Distance* (2021), Erica Dhawan, stated in her June 2021 BBC interview,

> When exchanging written messages – be it email or direct messages – you should also think carefully about the timing of your responses, and what that may say about your engagement with the project or person in question. You may not want to answer a query until you can do it justice, but the delay can seem like a lack of interest – resulting in sometimes intense anxiety.

In these cases, Dhawan suggests that you send an initial short-and-sweet reply to signal that you will give it consideration in due course.

Ultimately, Dhawan thinks that simply proofreading your messages to ensure that the meaning and the emotional subtext are as clear and appropriate as possible could turn out to save time and hassle in the future. David Robson wrote, in his article for BBC (2021), "When it comes to communicating carefully, less haste is more speed. It's a simple step, perhaps, but one that is regularly forgotten."

AVOID SAYING "I am going to call your mom!"

I worked with a teacher who would often threaten to call her students' moms. Because I heard this quite often, I started the habit myself when warning a student about their behavior. A new colleague heard me say this to a student. She privately asked me to stop saying this. She told me that she grew up without her mother, and my threatening statement might be insensitive to some students. I was deeply grateful for her comment - and honestly, a little embarrassed. I immediately stopped saying it. My colleague's comment also caused me to reflect on which parent I chose to call. When faced with the decision of which parent to connect with, email makes it easier because you can send a message to multiple recipients. With a phone call, teachers and administrators have to choose which parent to call. By knowing our students' home situations, we can hopefully use the correct terminology, such as sister, aunt, grandfather, guardian, etc., when referring to calling home. I approach this choice through a simple decision-making process:

1. Which parent has historically been in contact with you the most often? If you have a background with this parent, the conversation will be less awkward.

2. For parents you've never called before, investigate to learn more about their reputation. Which parent is the easiest to work with?

3. If a student doesn't live with both parents, do I need to balance how often each parent is contacted, or am I required by a court order to call both?

4. If you really do not know which parent to call, send an email to both and ask one of them (or both on a conference call) to contact you during a preset offering of times that you're available.

I do not always follow this advice because sometimes issues pop up at the end of the school day, and I need to reach a parent before I leave for the day. In such cases, I call one parent, then the other if I get voicemail. (Always leave a voicemail because it is scary to a parent to see the school's number on their caller ID without context.) In one instance, I called mom first and left a voicemail, but because I was eager to leave to go home, I forgot to call the dad. I followed up with an email to both. This typically would be fine but, in this case, the dad was bothered that I didn't call him because he was the primary contact for the child. (Truthfully, this information should have been available in our student information system.) I learned a lesson from this experience - call all the parents you can before sending an email saying, "I left you a voicemail."

FORMALITIES IN NAMES

"A rose by any other name would smell as sweet," is a popular line from Shakespeare's *Romeo and Juliet* (1597). Not all educators or parents would agree with that quote when it comes to addressing other adults by name. It's hard to know when it is appropriate to address parents with first names or last names. The answer to this dilemma depends on the school culture. Ask teachers who have worked there for a while. If you're still not sure, default to addressing parents by their last name during the first contact. It is important to use your student information system (SIS), if available, to verify titles such as Dr. and Mr., Ms., Drs., etc. Be aware of any bias when addressing parents. As cited in a Harvard Business Review IdeaCast episode "Anti-Bias Policies That Really Work in Customer Service" (Nickisch, 2021), white-sounding names tend to be addressed more often with honorifics. By taking the time to use the correct titles, you are demonstrating a level of respect that you also expect for yourself. I have worked in different schools that run across the spectrum of formality in communication. In some schools, parents, students, and teachers alike address each other more formally with last names. On the other side of the spectrum, even the kids address the teachers by their first name. Being called Ms.Crystal took some adjustment, but I eventually got used to it. This may seem like a trivial detail when building relationships is what really matters. I have, however, witnessed an incident where a teacher wrote an email addressing parents by their first names, and it turned out that the parents (both of whom were Drs.) were quite offended. It comes down to observing the school culture and being flexible to fit the norms of the community.

Another perspective on using titles when addressing parents came up in a November 2021 Tweet. The tweet author has asked to be identified as a math teacher in Seattle and board director for Washington Ethnic Studies Now.

Original Post
"It really bothers me when parents refer to me using my first name rather than Ms. _____. Names matter, I don't know you like that. Please refer to me as a professional. I go by Ms. _____ when I am teaching."

Reply
"I'm on the opposite end. When I work with parents, I am trying to develop a team to support their child. I don't want the separation of my formal name when they speak with me, yet they always refer to me as Mrs._____ to their child."

51

This tweet and its replies demonstrate the complexity of using or not using formalities when addressing other adults in a school setting. If in doubt, default to addressing parents with formalities unless told otherwise by the parent. If you sign emails using your last name, know that some parents won't take the hint and will still call you by your first name. Speak up, and gently remind them of your preferred name at your discretion.

BE SURE TO REPLY

Some parents use the lack of teacher replies as arguments when complaining to administration. It is very hard for an administrator to defend ignored emails. If you find that a parent is abusing the communication stream by emailing excessively, let your administrator know. Some schools also have a culture around blind carbon copy (BCC) and carbon copy (CC) on emails. If an administrator is CC'd on an email that is considered a minor issue, the parent may get the sense that the issue is more escalated than it really is.

There are times that email is a blessing, but it's also a curse. It's quick and convenient but can also pile up and become overwhelming. The German automobile company, Volkswagen, made international news in 2012 for turning off email delivery for their employees in the evenings (Keane, 2021), and in 2021 Portugal passed a law making it illegal for bosses to text their employees after hours (Gleeson, 2022). Email can follow us home, even on our phones if we let it. It's important to set boundaries on how frequently we are in contact with parents which is much easier said than done.

REFLECTION

- Thinking about how you spend your non-teaching hours, what proportion is dedicated to student feedback (grading), lesson planning, communication, and meetings? What needs to be adjusted? What is within your control to adjust?

- Do you have a dedicated time of day to check and reply to email or to make phone calls?

- What hesitations do you have about carving out parent communication time?

- What's your personal default when it comes to addressing other adults by first or last names?

Chapter 5
What about the difficult 10%?

No matter how many happy emails we send or how much we communicate professionally, there will always be a small percentage of parents who are grumpy or tricky. The common expression for the difficult portion of any population is 10%. Some school years it feels like you have more than 10% who are causing issues because they take up a disproportionate amount of your time compared to the 90% who are easy going.

As I wrote in the July 2020 Edutopia article, "A Strategy for Building Productive Relationships with Parents,"

> Some of these parents will be rude, overbearing, or poorly behaved because of factors that have nothing to do with you personally. Remain calm and kind, because you have no idea what life experiences they have been through, es-

pecially now as we all cope with the negative effects of Covid-19. That being said, you deserve to be treated with respect and should never allow verbal abuse.

I wrote this passage in the beginning months of the Covid-19 pandemic; however, the message remains true no matter when you're dealing with a difficult person at work. Their behavior often has nothing to do with you or your actions but, more likely, their own issues. When you factor in discussions about their children, strong emotions such as fear and anxiety bubble up to the surface. Some parents suffering from low self-confidence may become defensive; they perceive their parenting skills are being critiqued. Some parents who are dealing with a lot of stress at work and/or at home can lash out at the messenger because they feel powerless and overwhelmed.

Even though our work is personal, don't take difficult parents personally. We develop relationships with our students and we care deeply for them. We truly care about our students and their families. If a parent were to criticize your work, you might feel personally attacked.

A DIFFERENT PERSPECTIVE ON THE DIFFICULT PARENTS

In a Dallas Morning News 2016 opinion article, psychologists Robert Evans and Michael G. Thompson wrote,

> Many school administrators say most of the parents are fine. We believe them. But every school we visit – every single one – reports more frequent and more severe problems with parents. One small minority of parents are the most difficult: those who bully the school. These parents are habitually rude, demanding or disrespectful, engaging in personal attacks on teachers and administrators, demeaning and threatening them. They repeatedly violate the school's policies, values, and norms of conduct.

Although it may seem like many parents are quite similar to each other, it is important to see each parent as an individual, and avoid generalizing: *Those parents*. The language we use is important. If we use language to label parents in our conversations with colleagues, it can be hard to break out of the mindset that these parents are difficult. This creates a barrier to a future partnership. Just as we teach our students about fixed versus growth mindset in their academic work, we can practice the same approach to relationships with difficult parents.

This is easier said than done. A parent at our school was known for being a helicopter parent. She would email the teacher the same day as her son's test and ask how he did. If the teacher replied, she would shoot back numerous questions about his performance on the test. She even told teachers, "It is unacceptable for my son to have less than an A." (He was earning Cs.) While we all felt bad for the kid for being smothered like this, we also wanted to avoid this mom completely. The parent-teacher partnership was crumbling. However, it wasn't destroyed completely. One teacher took the time to meet with the mom face-to-face. She was empathetically firm in relaying realistic expectations for her son. The mom broke down in tears. She shared her own struggles with an ill family member, a lost job, and trying to raise her son amongst all of this stress. The meeting was incredibly productive. The mom's hovering decreased (it would be too much to expect for this behavior to cease completely), and this teacher became the unofficial point of contact for the mom. While this was an extra task for the teacher to take on, it was only temporary. The boy moved on to the next grade, and as he grew up, he developed more agency, and Mom developed more confidence.

I wish every story ended happily like this one. They don't, of course. But knowing that an empathetically firm talk with parents about managing expectations helped one family might give us hope for other families down the road.

Regardless of what issues are going on with the parents, our job as educators is to respect the parent relationship by offering clear, honest, and timely feedback about their child's progress. It is tempting to withhold information because you dread calling a parent who has historically been rude or irrational. Yvonne Bender, author of the 2005 book *The Tactful Teacher:*

Effective Communication with Parents, Colleagues, and Administrators, stresses that it is ok to disagree with a parent. This could be phrased as, "I'm afraid I can't agree with you, Jacinth. I just don't think it's a good idea for the Honor Society to hold an outdoor car wash in January." Use a respectful and firm tone to state your disagreement. Your job is to educate and care for your students – it is not to be a doormat to parents.

When you need to meet or call a parent who has a history of unpleasant interactions, ask an administrator or colleague to join in on the conversation. Having someone on your team during the meeting makes it harder for a parent to intimidate you. Ideally, tell the parent ahead of time that another person will be joining the call so they do not feel surprised. Consider a heads up such as, "I have invited Ms. Frizzle, our learning support specialist, to join our conversation this afternoon. She may be able to offer insights on strategies that may help Syed."

Another safety precaution is to greet the parent in a common area and wait for the third person to join before starting the meeting behind closed doors. A colleague of mine asked an administrator to join a meeting she predicted might become contentious. The administrator forgot about the meeting, and the teacher had to suffer through the meeting alone with the parent. Luckily, things didn't go as badly as she feared. If you do find yourself alone with a parent who doesn't pick up on the hints that the meeting is over or uses abusive language, position yourself between them and the door so you can leave the room if necessary.

YOU DO NOT HAVE TO TAKE ABUSE

As stated before we want to maintain professionalism and respect for all families. However, if you feel threatened or verbally abused you have the right to leave the situation immediately. Any administrator would support an employee who leaves a situation where they do not feel physically or psychologically safe. This is, hopefully, a rare event. There may be times that you may wish to politely end the meeting or step out. In one instance a colleague was meeting with two parents who were going through a difficult divorce. During the meeting, the focus shifted from talking about the student to the two parents bickering with each other. The teacher politely told the parents that she would step out for a moment so they could end their argument and return their focus to the meeting when she returned. The parents looked at her wide-eyed. They must have never been put in their place like that before. When she returned to the room, the parents meekly apologized to her and continued the conversation about their son.

Stories from the Field

Kimberly of Cary, NC
On my very first Meet the Teacher night after all parents had left, I had a dad come back to my room and back me against the wall and threaten me with physical violence if I didn't do everything I could to help his child who had an IEP. Once he left and I found someone, they told me very nonchalantly "Oh, he is banned from campus already." I was in a trailer out by the playground. No other room nearby. He didn't need to go through the building to get to me. And my admin didn't feel the need to warn me about this dad beforehand. It was a *great* way to start my career. I wish in my 19 years since I could say I have not had other similar situations, but that'd be a lie.

In another parent interaction, a young colleague of mine was being inappropriately challenged about her age and experience. The parent rudely asked her for her age. Maybe because of her inexperience or because she was taken aback by the inappropriate question, she answered his question. Later, as she recalled the story to us in the teachers' lounge, there was an overwhelming chorus of, "What! You don't have to answer that!"

Stories from the Field

Chuck of Munster, IN (currently Tracy, CA)
Back in my first year teaching (1987-88), I was teaching all electives but had a large number of seniors in my sociology class. This boy had done little to no work during the semester and had earned a failing grade. The father requested a meeting with me and the counselor. By failing the class the student was not going to graduate and could not even make up the credits in summer school. At that time, his only option was to come back in the fall to complete high school.

During the meeting, I explained the course, the requirements, and the missing assignments. The dad was visibly shaking and not interested in listening. His anger stayed for the entire meeting.

Near the end, after realizing his pleading and overt bullying was not going to work, he stood up and screamed that I, the teacher, was ruining his son's life. The counselor finished the meeting and escorted the father out of the room.

The counselor came back and tried to reassure me that everything was going to be all right and that I had done and said everything correctly.

I had coaching after school and got home late. My wife was at work so I checked the messages on my answering machine. That father had found my phone number and said again that I was ruining his son's life. He continued by telling me he not only knew where I worked but that he knew where I lived. That really shook me up. I had never experienced anything remotely like that.

The next day, I shared the message with the counselor and the principal. I even spoke with the superintendent of schools who said there was nothing he could do. I'm assuming that someone called and spoke to the father as I never heard from him again. That did not stop me from looking over my shoulder for quite some time.

A couple of years later I had the younger sister in class. I was more than a little nervous about having her in class. It turned out she was a far better student than her brother and did very well in the class. I never heard from the parents.

In the early days of my career, I worked at a school that required teachers to complete a form (in triplicate) as a record of any parent meeting. I never remembered to bring these forms with me when I met with a parent. I probably couldn't have found them in my file cabinet even if I had looked. In parent meetings, I talked to the parents and jotted down a few notes, but mostly, we just talked. I felt the discussion would have suffered if it was bogged down by a regimented form. But the problem was the lack of documentation. Remember, email was not as common in the year 2000 where I was teaching as it is today. I had no way of communicating to parents a summary of what we discussed in the meeting (except for that darned triplicate form).

The required carbon triplicate form was, in my opinion, ridiculous, which probably subconsciously caused me to lose the forms or forget them. I was a young teacher back then who lacked the confidence to speak up about a better solution. Decades later, I speak up much more often – some might say too often. My advice to new teachers is to respectfully offer suggestions if you spot a process or policy that could be improved. As an administrator, I welcomed suggestions for change and improvement from all teachers from all levels of experience. I wish I had spoken up back then.

ATTACKS ON YOUR SUBJECT CONTENT

Parents who are concerned about the content their children are learning in school is not a new issue for educators. Parents have raised concerns about schools teaching sex education, drug-use prevention education, "new" math, social emotional education, or religious teachings (or lack of) for decades and decades. The hot debate over Critical Race Theory (CRT) being taught in schools came to the surface along with the widespread protests after the murders of George Floyd, Breonna Taylor, and Ahmaud Arbery in 2020. Concerned parent groups popped up in school districts around the country in reaction to the heightened awareness of racial injustice in our country. In some areas of the US, legislation was passed dictating what teachers could teach regarding race and racism. According to Brookings (Gibbons, 2021), some of the content that was banned in 2020 included texts by particular authors or on certain topics, perspectives of enslaved or indigenous peoples in telling the history of the United States, and any other content that might be perceived to run counter to the white and/or Christian narrative in literature and history.

If you have been challenged directly by a parent regarding the content you teach, you may feel as if the parent-teacher relationship is strained beyond repair. In response to such challenges, I highly recommend reading Angela Watson's September 2021 article "How to respond if a parent accuses you of teaching Critical Race Theory." A helpful tip that Watson offers in this article is to solely address parent feedback that directly concerns you and your teaching.

> ..make sure you are focused on addressing concerns brought directly to you or your administrative team. It may not be worthwhile to address gossip and rumors or to be part of an online community or parent group that frequently complains about the school system.

She ends the article with a message of hope for maintaining a partnership with the parents. Reassure parents that you are not telling their children what to think, but rather, how to think. Listening to and analyzing a variety of perspectives is an important skill for students to learn. Watson also suggests reminding parents that the door is always open for communication – tell parents you welcome their questions and viewpoints. Be prepared to offer helpful resources to parents such as *So You Want to Talk About Race* by Ijeoma Oluo. (2018), *Between the World and Me* by Ta-Nehisi Coates (2015), or Ibram X. Kendi's *How to Be an Anti-Racist* (2019). As more and more books and media about racial injustice are being published, keep up to date on relevant resources to offer parents and colleagues.

Even after you explain your common ground or offer resources, some parents will still be unconvinced that your intentions are positive for their child. We can only continue to learn and teach your curriculum equitably to all of your students. There will always be the 10%.

FOLLOW UP IN WRITING

Email shouldn't replace face-to-face meetings or phone calls, but it sure does make follow up more efficient. If you haven't already, start the practice of sending an email after each phone call or meeting. To keep the admin in the loop, copy the appropriate administrator (CC or BCC depending on the nature of the conversation) summarizing what was discussed and what plan of action each party will take. Here is an example of a follow-up email:

> *Mr. Holland,*
> *Thank you for taking the time to meet with me today regarding Opus's behavior in class. As we discussed, Opus will stay after school tomorrow to clean desks as his consequence for writing on the school furniture. I appreciate your support and collaboration.*

Such a follow up helps you and the administrators to keep record of previous communication with parents in case another incident occurs again.

THE DIFFICULT REQUESTS FROM WELL-INTENTIONED PARENTS

Sometimes, it's not the parent who is being difficult, but rather the request itself is difficult. While we want to work with parents to meet the needs of the student, some requests are not always best for their child's educational experience. The following questions have been asked of my colleagues and myself many times from parents. After each request is a suggestion for how to say no firmly but kindly. I have phrased these requests in a cheeky way for humor's sake. Most of the time these requests are a bit ridiculous, but there are times that these requests are valid due to health, family situations, or other extreme circumstances. Because fair doesn't mean equal, you can certainly give a student more time on an assignment or another exception because of a family crisis but not give the same extension to another student for a much less serious reason. If a student or parent ever questions the fairness of a request (which I find is rare), I always tell them that another student's situation is not something I can share.

"**Since there are two days left in the grading period, is there anything my child can do to earn extra credit or bring up their average?**"

<u>Communicate as early as possible</u> *with parents if there is a chance for a student to improve their average. If a parent contacts you about improving a grade with only a few days left in the grading period, you can reiterate to the parents that all of the planned assessments have been completed for the term and offer tips on how their*

child can get a strong start in the upcoming term.

"My child was up late playing a sport, celebrating his second cousin's roommate's graduation, practicing the bassoon, or some other reason why they are unable to take the test you announced weeks ago. Can they take the test scheduled for today at another time?"

<u>Stand firm on this one</u> *unless there are extreme extenuating circumstances. Offer to answer any last minute questions if there is time before school or between classes. Reassure the parent that there have been x number of review days to prepare students for the assessment. If this request comes as an email, you could also reply to it after their child has taken the test, making it a moot point.*

"Can my child turn in his work late?" See the above reasons.

<u>Inevitably a student will need to turn in an assignment late now and again.</u> *Life happens. To avoid handling this request on a case-by-case basis, I set up a freebie system for daily work in*

71

my middle school classes. Each term every stu-dent gets an exemption from a daily assignment - no questions asked. They are responsible for practicing the material in time for the next as-sessment, but they do not have to hand it in. If a parent requests that another assignment during the term be handed in late, then I can have a conversation about why they have missed TWO daily assignments. Parents are less likely to push back when there might be a pattern developing around missed daily work. I taught my students to use their freebie thoughtfully. They should plan ahead for an upcoming late-night event, birthday, or another busy day.

"My child is unable to attend any of the tutorial sessions you offer. Are you available every day after 8 pm or before 7 am to help her with her homework?"

<u>Reiterate to the parent which days/times you are available for extra help.</u> *If their child has questions outside of the offered times, list out the resources that are available to them such as notes, the textbook, online resources, contacting a classmate, or (if you have the time) make a short video of yourself explaining the concept*

that they can watch at any time. To avoid this is-
sue altogether, my school's math department
scheduled one math teacher to be on duty every
morning and every afternoon for tutorials. If a
student had a math question, they could pop in
before or after school to ask a question - they
may not have been able to see their own math
teacher, but at least they could get their ques-
tion answered.

"I see that my child left her science project on the kitchen table. Can I bring it to school so that she won't lose credit?"

<u>Some schools are clear about not allowing par-</u>
<u>ents to deliver homework and projects</u> *to*
school. There are various reasons for this - one
being equity and another being to teach kids
responsibility. If your school does not have a
policy regarding parents delivering assignments
to their children, then it is very difficult to pre-
vent this as an individual teacher. If it is impor-
tant to you that students are not allowed to ac-
cept school day deliveries from parents, there
are steps you can take to prevent it.

 ✳ <u>Set an expectation at Parent Night</u> *that*
  parents are NOT expected to bring for-

gotten assignments to school. Stress the importance of responsibility and equity in your reasoning. Most parents will be relieved that this is not expected or acceptable.

✳ <u>**Set a rolling due date for major projects.**</u> *For example, the science project is due the week of Sept 20. This is a smoke and mirrors tactic to hide the fact that the real due date is the Friday of that week but you'll accept projects starting Monday. (This also makes grading more manageable because projects trickle in over a five-day range.)*

✳ <u>**Do not allow a student to call their parents from school to request homework/ project delivery.**</u> *The older students might sneak an email or text to ask their parents to bring an assignment, but you can discourage this by reiterating to students that asking parents to deliver their work promotes inequality and irresponsibility. (They probably won't care but at least you shared your two cents.)*

"My child would prefer to be in Mr. Feeney's class, or my child needs to be in advanced-level math, or my child prefers to take English in the mornings, can she switch classes?"

Hopefully, your school has a policy regarding how a student places into leveled classes. *If this is the case, refer the parent back to the posted policy of requirements. If the class change request is not related to a leveled class, this is something that can be immediately escalated to the administration.*

"My child does not get along with Trouble Jones, Jr. Can you make sure they do not socialize together during the school day?"

Kids move in and out of friendships *like a Houston driver changes lanes on I-10. One day they are best friends, and the next day they call each other stupid smelly-face. It is ok to ask two students who are having a rough patch to give each other space because, as the educator, you can observe the temperature of their relationship every day. Parents are not close to what's happening with friendships on the playground at recess. Parents also often only hear one side of the story. Reassure parents that students are closely monitored and that they are taught restorative practices and conflict resolution. Parents might need assurance that mistreatment is never tolerated, but also we want to keep the path clear for a potential repair in their friendship. If a parent is worried about their child being bullied or physically harmed (even if it is an unjustified concern), stay in frequent communication with the concerned parent so they can feel confident that their child is safe and happy at school.*

WHEN PARENTS GO OVER YOUR HEAD

One of the worst feelings you can get as a teacher is when your supervisor asks to speak with you with no context as to what the discussion will be about. If you are anything like me, your mind meanders through possible scenarios: What did I say wrong? Did I upset a student? Oftentimes, these meetings are benign topics like, "Can you cover lunch duty next week?" (By the way, if you are an administrator reading this, stop asking for an appointment to talk with a teacher without context. Just don't do it – it's too anxiety-inducing.)

But there are also the dreaded moments when an administrator wants to talk with you because of a parent complaint. In an ideal world, the administrator will tell the parent that they want the teacher to be the first point of contact for a concern. But, in the defense of administrators, some adamant parents refuse to go to the teacher first no matter how much they are encouraged by the administrator. (Also in an ideal world, the administrator will identify who made the complaint. If they won't or can't, express how important transparency is to you as a matter of professional respect.)

When this happens, it is hard to not feel betrayed by the parent. Are they so afraid of retribution that they can't speak to you directly? Ask your administrator what they think is the best way to react to the complaint. Should you reach out to the parents directly? How should you change any interactions with the child knowing the parents complained about your class? As educators, we know we absolutely cannot hold any blame on children for their parents' actions. If you have been teaching a while, you have most likely had a parent complain to the administration about ridiculous is-sues - here are a few of mine: I once said that boys and girls can wear make-up if they want to (I stand by this as truth), I give too much home-work (this one might've had some truth to it, but I am better about that now), I talk about religion too much in class (this one is completely made up), and I answer student questions with ques-tions (totally true).

While it is very upsetting to learn that a parent complained behind your back, listen to the complaint with curiosity and openness. There might be some truth to what was said - and maybe you firmly stand behind your actions, or maybe you reflect on what you could improve in your class.

REFLECTION

- Think of a difficult parent you have inter-acted with in your career. How could having a reframe of the situation change how you interacted and felt about the exchange?

- What do you wish your school adminis-trators would do to support you with difficult parents? Have you addressed this wish with the administration at your school?

- What factors might hinder a teacher from standing firm when disagreeing with a parent? Describe scenarios when it is appropriate to yield to a parent's request and when a teacher should absolutely refuse a parent's request.

Chapter 6
What if I am wrong?

As an eighth grade teacher, I received a polite email from a parent asking about a few low grades that I had entered in the gradebook for their daughter. It struck me as odd because this student hardly ever earned low grades. Shortly into my investigation, I began to get that sweaty, prickly feeling that you get when you know you messed up. I had inadvertently typed another student's grades in for her. Essentially, I skipped a line in the online grade book. I felt sick. How could I have let this happen? My small error could have affected her report card, honor roll status, and National Junior Honor Society. I began to journey down the meandering dark wormhole of worry. The only choice I had was to own my mistake and start eating crow. I told my administrator about my error as a heads up in case the parents became very upset. Then, I told the parents of my error and that I would fix it immediately. I was certain they would think I was an incompetent teacher who isn't careful in her work. In reality, my worry was for nothing (as usual). The parents understood and thanked me for fixing the error. Not all parents would react this way, of course. Even if they had become upset and thought less of me, I couldn't go back in time and change anything. The only thing I could do was fix my mistakes and try to learn from them.

WHEN TO RETEACH OR OFFER RETAKES ON ASSESSMENTS

An administrator once told me, "If a few students aren't doing the homework, then it's on them. If almost all of your students aren't doing the homework, then it's on you." I think of this when a majority of my students do not perform well on an assessment. From time to time, a teacher will also lament to me, "I spoon-fed them exactly what material to study, and they still failed!" It is so hard when you KNOW, as a teacher, that you taught the material well, and you gave the students a thorough review, but they just didn't click with the assessment. Our thoughts can go one of two directions:

1. They obviously didn't study, and they deserve their poor grades.

OR

2⃝ I have to look at this assessment objectively and reconsider some factors in how the
material was received by the students.

By offering a redo on the assessment or test
corrections towards earning a better grade,
some teachers might feel as if this is admitting a
fault in their teaching. Even the best of educators have to take a hard look at certain assessments, so rest assured, you're not alone in this.
An excellent teacher with over 40 years of experience told me that he once graded a class set
of tests that were terrible. He realized that the
students needed to be retaught the material. He
held the stack of graded papers up in front of
his anxiously awaiting students – then surpris-
ingly, dropped the entire stack in the wastebasket. The students erupted in applause once they
got over their initial shock. He explained to his
students, "Something was amiss with this test so
we are starting over." (The wastebasket drop
was added for dramatic effect.) Because this
was the first and only time this teacher has done
something like this, it definitely caught the kids'
attention. By admitting that a reteach was nec-

essary, he established trust and respect with his students. When we admit to our kids that we made a mistake, they can see the human side of us. Revealing vulnerability takes strength. If you are a Dr. Brené Brown fan, you might know a lot about vulnerability in leadership. If vulnerability scares you, stop reading this book, and go find a book, podcast, or Ted Talk by Brené Brown right this second!

GIVE YOURSELF GRACE

You will make mistakes, that's a fact, but remind yourself that you did the best you could do at the time. It has been said that teachers make more than a thousand decisions every day. Many of these decisions are on the spot, under pressure, and without enough information. Some of these decisions might not be to the liking of a student or parent. Perhaps, some of these decisions have even been a mistake. At the end of the day, there may be a lingering decision that just doesn't sit well. Reflect on that feeling. What could you have done differently? What can be done to redirect the course of that decision? If it was the right decision, who do you need to talk to to help yourself feel at ease with the choice? Part of my role as an assistant division head was to check which parents had completed the COVID safety app every morning. At the beginning of the school year, I sent a canned, slightly reprimanding, but mostly polite email to all non-compliant parents. Because I was new to the safety app system, I mistakenly sent emails to parents who had in fact completed the app. I cannot even remember how many apology replies I sent that day. I am sorry I mistakenly sent you the email, and additionally, I am sorry I reprimanded you for something you didn't do. It was a rough start to the school year.

REALIZE WHEN YOU HAVE GONE TOO FAR

A good friend and colleague of mine joked around with his students a lot. He was one of those fun, goofy teachers the kids adored. His jokes with the kids seemed to be positively accepted by his students, even if they were edgy. At one point, he gave a student the nickname Smelldon. The kid seemed to like it, the rest of the class called him that too. Smelldon's mom expressed to the teacher that, in fact, he did not like the nickname and was too embarrassed to say anything. My teacher friend was mortified. He had no idea the impact this nickname had on this boy. He apologized privately to the student and told the class that he would be called by his real name from then on. Kudos to the mom for going to the teacher, not straight to the administration. And kudos to the teacher for admitting fault and taking swift action to rectify the situation. I hope someone followed up to check that this student felt satisfied with the resolution.

One of my many weaknesses is trying to prove I am right all of the time. When I meet with parents whose point of view does not align with the facts I have to consciously check myself to not go into "I am right, damn it!" mode. I get this way especially when a parent complains about a colleague. As an administrator, I wanted to protect my teachers from pesky, nagging parents when I knew the teacher was working hard and doing amazing things in the classroom. To avoid slipping into this mode, I had to remind myself that the parents might only be hearing their child's side of the story. Sometimes, a 10-year-old doesn't report an accurate or comprehensive account of a lesson or assignment. I bring evidence to these meetings and hold my tongue when an opinion wants to burst out of my mouth. Unfortunately for my family, I save all of these opinions and "I am right, damn it!" comments for when I can vent in the privacy of my home.

When you are in the wrong in a situation, there is a parade of emotions that comes marching through your thoughts. "Will I look like a fool?" "I can't face the parents because I feel humiliated." "Will these parents ever trust me again?" And maybe even, "Will I get fired for this?" Not all teacher behavior can be apologized away, of course. There is a small percentage of teachers who make egregious decisions that will cost them their job, and perhaps, rightly so. However, if you are a well-intentioned educator who cares about your students, there will be times that you will make missteps that aren't disastrous. When this happens we have to step up and speak up. Here are a few sentences that might stop the parade of emotions and help you move forward from the situation.

After reviewing my records again,
it seems that I misspoke regarding...
Thank you for bringing this to my attention.
Let me research this and get back to you.

Thank you for sharing your concern with me.
It certainly was not my intention to _____,
but I now see how this may have been per-
ceived.

It sounds like Sydney told you XYZ
happened in class. I spoke with Mr. Lee
and here is a printout of the activity you
are referencing.

You're not perfect. The parents aren't perfect. The kids aren't perfect. We will all make mistakes and have to apologize from time to time. The best thing you can do is provide an atmosphere of grace and learning in your classroom for your kids and yourself.

OVERSTEPPING YOUR BOUNDS

A principal I worked with used to say, "I can't tell families what to do in their own living room."
I've never forgotten this when I desperately want to tell parents what they should be doing

at home. It's easy to want to nudge parents to-ward what we think is the correct way to raise children. We all come from different upbring-ings with widely varying expectations. We can-not help but look through our own biased lens at the way a parent is choosing to raise their child.

A few rules of thumb that I have learned, from the wise principal quoted earlier, have helped me navigate the boundaries of home and school.

- **We can expect students to do their own work at home.** If we suspect a parent or caregiver has completed their work for them, educators can question it, but be careful about trying to prove it. (In fact, some educators make all major grade as-signments and projects in-class only to avoid this issue altogether.)

- **We can expect students to talk to their parents respectfully in our presence.** If a student is sassing their parents while you're there with them in a conversation, you can tell the student, "Here at school, you will speak to everyone, including your parents, respectfully."

- **If your school allows delivery of assignments, lunches, or other forgotten items, we can choose not to deliver the item to the child right away.** Some administrators feel quite strongly about this policy because of the issues of equity. Not all families have the means or flexibility to deliver homework, water bottles, or science projects to the school. Only privileged students get this luxury. A caveat here: If a child forgets a lunch box, the school must provide a lunch for every child who doesn't have a lunch. Necessary personal items such as change of clothes or medical needs will always be acceptable for parent delivery.

- **We can expect parents to respect the rules of the school regarding communication during the school day.** If there is a school rule that students cannot use their phones during the day, this also means parent calls and texts are prohibited. In my experience, almost every time that a ringing phone interrupts my class, it is a call from the student's parent.

BEING AWARE OF BIASES

As a white female educator, my writings about my experiences around inclusion and race in schools will come from a perspective of privilege. Because of the limited lens of my experiences, for this section I sought out many references written by other authors who can speak about inclusion and race with a voice rooted in experience.

I have worked with some educators over the decades who claim to "not see color." As a result, they are not seeing the culture and identities of their students. Susie An wrote a 2019 NPR article, "Changing Classrooms: When Students are Black and Teachers are White," in which she interviewed consultant Dr. Aaron Griffen. "You will have individuals who will say 'I don't see color. I don't see race. I only see children.' That, for me, is an excuse that you're not willing to change what you're doing to meet the needs of children." Griffen said.

One way to start to meet the needs of our children is to acknowledge the experiences of the students of color in our schools. White educators teaching in schools that have a student body with a majority of white students must hold space to listen to how a student of color feels being "the only" or "one of very few."

A 2020 USA Today article "I'm a white teacher with a classroom of minority students. Here's how I teach across race." by Larry Strauss states, "Unfortunately, [...] the vast majority of students of color attend schools in which the demographics of the teachers do not match those of the students. In some cases, the disparity is extreme."

A problematic bias that teachers need to examine is how often and for what reasons we are contacting parents. Melinda D. Anderson writes, in her 2016 article for "The Atlantic" "How Discrimination Shapes Parent-Teacher Communication," about how teacher communication with parents of varying races might differ because of implicit bias.

Betina Hsieh, an assistant professor of teacher education at California State University in Long Beach, expressed that schools that prepare teachers to be educators should help teacher candidates "understand these troubling disparities and… racial stereotypes" to promote better communication between parents and teachers in general. "A lot of [my students] are young, and the great majority are white… It often doesn't occur to them to contact parents on a proactive basis, and many of them are intimidated to talk to parents," she said. Toss race and ethnicity into the equation, and "it heightens [their] concerns that they'll 'get it wrong'… so some of them don't even want to try at all." As a systemic issue, starting in teacher education is critical, she notes, but the work is also in "pushing teachers to consider their roles in upholding systems that can be unjust to various communities of color – disproportionately Latino and black students." Considering the words of Professor Hsieh, examine your own parent communication with families of all races and backgrounds in your classes. Are there some parents who are contacted more often for negative reasons? Are there some parents who are contacted more often for any reason at all?

If you are a middle school teacher or parent, you might have heard of the 2019 award-winning graphic novel *New Kid* by Jerry Craft (2019). The book's main character, Jordan Banks, is a black seventh grader who is a new kid at a predominately white private school. Throughout the book, he is consistently called the wrong name by his teachers. The audience for this book is geared toward middle school age, but educators can gain a lot from reading about Jordan's experience. Mahnaz Dar, Reference and Professional Reading Editor for Library Journal and School Library Journal (2019), writes,

> *New Kid*'s lessons about race and privilege aren't just for young people. Educators have much to learn from Jordan's story… And African American teachers have told Craft that their white colleagues still get their names wrong, even after years of working at a school. He hopes that the teachable moments in the book will push adult readers to recon-

sider their own biases. "Take that extra second. Learn someone's name. Have a conversation. Look them in the eye."

KNOWING WHEN TO PASS THE BUCK

A teacher once reported to me that she witnessed a middle school girl hit another at recess. This was baffling to the teacher because the girls were known to be best friends. When the teacher asked what happened, the girl who hit her friend said that the friend accidentally bumped her with her backpack, and it really hurt. She reacted with a hit. As these two girls sat in my office, I realized that this is a case of a middle schooler reacting without thinking. I told each girl that I would be calling their parents but there would be no severe consequences from this incident. I was in for quite a surprise when I called one of the parents. The parent of the child who was hit was livid. The conversion included accusations of bullying, an unsafe school environment, administrators underplaying violence, and even a quick mention of how much money the parent had donated to the school. The conversation went completely off the rails. There was nothing I could say to calm this parent down. That's when I knew I had to pass the buck.

Passing the buck means shifting responsibility to another party. This doesn't have to mean escalating to your supervisor. Sometimes, another colleague can help. In this case, I knew that the student's homeroom teacher had a long relationship with this parent. She would have much better success talking with this irate parent. I asked the teacher if she would mind calling the parent to reassure them that their child was not bullied by her best friend and that we did have a safe environment during recess. It was a risky move, but luckily, it was successful. The teacher and parent's close relationship over the school year had allowed them to establish a trust that I did not have with the parent. Without that trust, this parent and I were not going to have a productive conversation. This was a humbling experience for me because I really thought this was a cut and dry situation that I could easily handle. It is important to know when you're not the right person for a particular job.

REFLECTION

- Think of a time that you became frustrated or angry at a person via email or phone, such as a difficult customer service interaction. What emotions were you experiencing? How did you feel after the interaction? Were other things going on in your life that may have contributed to the frustration of this particular situation?

- What have you been wrong about that you had to apologize for? How did you learn from this experience?

- Take a look at your own implicit biases around race and culture other than your own? How are they affecting your work with parents?

- How do you know when to handle a parent interaction yourself and when to pass it on to a colleague who would be more successful communicating in this instance?

Chapter 7

Hard conversations

Some conversations are going to be harder than others. Sometimes, you have to tell a parent something unsettling or upsetting about their child. It's tempting to sweep such news under the rug because no one likes to give bad news. As empathetic people, we want to avoid causing discomfort for others, but if we do not dive in and tell parents tough news, their child could end up worse for it. Executive Leadership Coach, Jel Garfinkle, suggests in the 2017 "Harvard Business Review" article "How to Have Difficult Conversations When You Don't Like Conflict," trying to reframe your mindset as you prepare for tough conversations. Garfinkle offers these tips, "Begin from a place of curiosity and respect, and stop worrying about being liked. Focus on what you're hearing, not what you're saying. Be direct. Don't put it off. Expect a positive outcome." Even if you prepare thoroughly and directly deliver the news, there is always the chance that parents can react in a negative way. Some may get angry, some may be sad, and some will stay in denial. If you fear that a parent might become aggressive with you, refer to chapter 5 for ideas for working with tough parent interactions.

SENSITIVE CONVERSATIONS

A good friend and colleague decided long ago that she will not call any parent unless someone makes her do it. I was curious why she was so adamant about this stance because sometimes, calling on the phone takes much less time and energy than emailing. She shared that long ago she called a mom with a relatively mild concern. The mom flew off the handle and began to berate my friend. That was enough to make the teacher swear off phone calls forever, which is a shame.

Making a phone call about a sensitive topic can make any educator nervous. If you feel like the nature of the conversation is beyond your scope as a teacher, ask the school counselor, an administrator, or nurse for help. I once had a teen student in my class who did not wear deodorant. It was becoming a problem because the odor was disturbing the nearby students.

How do you broach the subject of body odor with parents? This is certainly too sensitive for an email and awkward for a phone call. Fortunately, I worked with an amazing team of nurses who made the parent contact for me. Other sensitive topics include repeating foul language or actions to a parent (now, I am less afraid of this, I let the words fly out!), admitting to a mistake you made (see chapter 6), and other behaviors that will greatly upset the parents ("Your child touched another child inappropriately."). None of these are easy scenarios. But it gets easier if you seek support, be clear and objective in your description, and always come from a place of empathy.

Regardless of your experience with students with learning differences, avoid suggesting a diagnosis to parents. Double-check with your school's learning specialist on the policy of suggesting testing and diagnoses. You may objectively share with parents what you are observing in class. Speak about specific, observable behaviors such as the student needs several reminders to stay in their seat, they perform better on classwork when they have more time, or they have three missing assignments. If you keep your feedback objective, parents have concrete information to share with a diagnostician, psychologist, or healthcare professional. If you are not qualified and authorized to make a diagnosis, don't.

On the flip side, if the parent seems overly shocked or worried about their child's behavior, it can be reassuring to tell parents that the behavior is developmentally appropriate. This is not to say that the behavior is condoned, rather it is not atypical. Knowing what is developmentally appropriate for their grade level is knowledge that comes with experience. If you're not sure if the behavior is developmentally appropriate, check in with experienced colleagues. To further illustrate this point, I called a parent when their seventh grader shared test answers with a classmate. The parent was appalled and overly worried. I assured the mom that her child would be serving a consequence for academic dishonesty AND that this is an excellent learning opportunity. The student was not the first seventh grader to ever cheat. Making mistakes and learning from them is a normal part of growing up. The mom was very relieved to hear this.

WHEN YOU'RE NEW AND PARENTS RESIST THE CHANGE

"That's not how things are done here."

"Mrs. Smith did this differently."

"You gave a quiz on the day before Christmas break?! That's not what WE do."

It's hard being new. Learning a new culture but still being yourself is a delicate balancing act. Sometimes, even the smallest actions can rub against the culture of the school without you even knowing. For example, when I gave my first partner quiz, some people I worked with flipped out. They had never heard of collaborative assessments.

If you sense that something you want to implement might counter the current culture, ease into the change. Communicate, communicate, communicate. Explain to your parents, students, and colleagues why you want to give a collaborative assessment or whatever new addition you want to implement. Explain the benefits, including citations of research, for everyone involved. If you sense there is some nervousness, offer that this is a pilot run to see how it works.

When my school hired a new administrator, he was deliberate with which changes he wanted to implement so that the community didn't suffer from severe change whiplash. One of his few changes the first year was restructuring the parent conferences. I was one of the vocal naysayers. "Wait! What? Why are you fixing what isn't broken?!" He handled naysayers like me with patience and understanding. He explained carefully how the new structure worked at his last school, and he even had answers to all of the potential problems that might arise with the newly proposed structure. Best of all, he offered the plan as a pilot to test it out. Despite my concerns and pesky naysaying, the parent conferences were a success! Because he took the time to build relationships and carefully listen to concerns from the community, the new structure was set up for success because we felt heard and, as a result, more willing to try something new.

If you have ever started teaching a class mid-year, the pushback on change can be even worse. Bringing in a new teacher part way through the year is disruptive for students and parents alike, especially if the class already has a good flow and routine. The pushback is more understandable in these situations. You will hear far too often, "Mr. Jones did it this way!" From the start, outline what will change and what will remain the same. Make a video that parents can watch so that they can hear your tone and see your body language. Mention what aspects of Mr. Jones' class will stay to reassure families who are afraid of the change. Explain how you will implement your personal talents and strengths to enhance the learning environment. No two teachers will ever be exactly alike – no one can reasonably expect that. But not every-one is reasonable when stressed by change. Have an excess of grace and understanding during a transition while balancing professional boundaries.

One thing I have noticed while working in schools is that some educators and administrators do not see a difference between pushback and blowback. Pushback means that one or a few parents will express a concern about a change. Blowback means several or more parents will find the new change completely unacceptable. Pushback is to be expected and can be managed. If you are considering a change in which parent pushback is expected, be ready to back-up the decision with strong reasons. Maybe even get in front of the pushback by explaining the reasons for the change in a mass communication along with the announcement of the change. The reasons may not suit the parent who is pushing back, but by pulling back the curtain to be more transparent maybe some of the pushback will be prevented.

WHEN PARENTS BELIEVE A RIDICULOUS CLAIM

I worked with a very wise nun at a progressive Catholic school who started her parent presentation with the famous saying, "We will believe half of what we hear about your home if you will believe half of what you hear about school." You probably have to be wise, and maybe even a nun, to get away with such a statement with some persnickety parents. *(Disclaimer here: this section is referring only to misinterpreted meanings of what was said at school. If a child reports a claim of abuse, take it very seriously, and report it to the appropriate authorities immediately.)*

Of course, we always value what kids say, but sometimes, they hear something you said and take away a completely different meaning. Hopefully, a parent will approach such an incident directly with you and not go over your head. I do not understand why some parents go straight to an administrator to ask about what a teacher meant by something they said - how is the administrator supposed to know what the teacher said and meant? If the parent does question a statement from their child, don't get defensive. Consider the age of the child. Even eighth graders misinterpret what is said. My own child (age 14 at the time of this writing) told me that her teacher doesn't allow her to ask questions in class. My first thought as an educator was "Bullsh*t! No teacher doesn't allow questions. Teachers love questions! Clearly you're mistaken." Instead, I asked my child, "Why do you say that?" She replied, "She won't allow questions during tests." Ah-ha! There's the real story. If a parent can't get to the bottom of the story with their child at home, try replying, "I can see how he could take that message away. Thank you for letting me know. I will circle back with him to clarify what I intended." Then, take the time to circle back to the child to clarify what you meant. No matter how much we have repeated the same message to kids, some will interpret the meaning differently. It is well worth the time to listen to the parent's concern and try again with the child to make sure you are all on the same page.

REFLECTION

- Has anyone had a difficult conversation with you? How did they address the sensitive topic? What could they have done differently?

- Have you initiated a difficult conversation with someone, telling your boss you're leaving your job, critiquing the work of an employee, breaking up with a partner, revealing something deeply personal to a loved one? How did you feel before, during, and after the conversation?

- What advice do you have for someone approaching a difficult conversation?

- What are some ways to avoid becoming defensive even in the face of a ridiculous argument?

Chapter 8

How to communicate with parents with varying levels of engagement

With all things in life, there can be too much of a good thing. As mentioned in previous chapters, there will be parents who are far too involved in a negative, contentious way. Alternatively, there will be parents who take up a disproportionate amount of a teacher's time with the best of intentions. How can educators build healthy partnerships with parents of all levels of engagement ranging from the hard to reach to the hard to manage?

OVERLY HELPFUL

This section might seem hypocritical. We want parents to be engaged and supportive, so why would we reject any offers of help? At the very beginning of the Covid-19 Pandemic, when my school shut down, like most educators, my classes continued 100% online. A parent reached out to me to offer to go grocery shopping for me. (You may recall that grocery stores had a limited selection of items, and lines were long due to limited capacity requirements.) Her reasoning was that while I was dedicating my time to teaching her child online, she wanted to help me in return. This gesture sticks in my memory as one of the most generous offers from a parent I have ever received. I expressed how grateful I was for her offer, but I politely declined her offer for a couple of reasons:

1 I didn't want to cross the professional line by giving a parent my grocery list (...and if you can pick up some Twizzlers and a six-pack of Coors Light, that'd be great!)

2 I didn't know how far this generosity would go in our parent-teacher relationship.

The professional line is very hard to draw and even harder to stick to. Once, a parent brought me a casserole when my baby was sick. It was very sweet of her, but she had my home number and address and saw me in slouchy, spit-up-stained lounge clothes when she dropped off the casserole. Not something that every student's parent gets or wants to see.

These are extreme examples that involve a teacher's home life, but overeager parents can also potentially cross a line at school as well. Parents who plan parties well beyond what is reasonable for school can be hard to rein in. (I once heard of a room-parent catering an elementary party with sushi. Whose school party budget allowed that? What percentage of elementary kids appreciate or even like sushi?) Parents who want to see a particular club or program offered at school can cross a line as well. As a former math club sponsor, a dad asked me to consider having the math club join a large-scale national math competition. He was quite enthusiastic about this particular competition, and he even volunteered his time to help sponsor the club. His offer to volunteer was, of course, contingent on the club participating in the competition of his choosing. A few red flags were raised here: do we want a parent attending math club, especially considering the well-being of the club members who struggle? Is this particular math competition a good fit for the culture of our math club? Can we rely on this dad to consistently attend club meetings? And for how long? In the end, I gently told this eager dad that we would look into bringing in math problems from the math competition, but we were not going to commit fully to signing up for the formal competition. He was disappointed that I did not accept his offer to help, but I knew this was the best decision for our club.

Managing parent involvement can come in the form of a well-meaning parent volunteering to be a guest speaker. Yes, we want to have parents volunteering their time and talents to the school. But we want to welcome parent guest speakers strategically. Do they have a presentation outline they can submit for approval? Is the topic in line with the school's mission and curriculum? If you do get a very zealous parent asking to volunteer, but you're not sure where their volunteerism will fit in, ask for backup. Refer this parent to the school administrative assistant(s), PTA, instructional coaches, or another non-teaching department to ask for their help in placing this parent. It is a tough position to be in when you want to welcome parent help, but organizing that help is becoming another chore for you.

Another example of overly helpful parents can come by way of too frequent communication. These might be emails to just check in or the random pop-in (see chapter 9). I remember once eating lunch in the school cafeteria, and a parent who was substitute teaching that day came by my table to ask how her daughter did on a test – a test given that morning! I finished chewing my food then politely replied that I would hand tests back to the students once I'd had a chance to grade them. It is hard to get upset when a well-intentioned parent wants to connect, but it is up to us as educators to set appropriate boundaries. If you find that a parent is getting too cozy with you in their communication, one tactic to try is to delay your replies to emails. Write back after 24 hours for each message in the thread. This will lessen the constant *ding* of emails from the parent who treats email like it's a chat.

If you have ever seen the ABC sitcom, *The Goldbergs*, you may remember the mom, Bev Goldberg. She is a proud mother of three who is known for popping into her children's high school often to "offer her help and advice" by telling the administration how to do their jobs. In Season 8 Episode 11 (Davidson, 2021) of *The Goldbergs*, Bev invites her youngest son's teachers over for a surprise field day. Needless to say, teenage Adam is not happy with this.

> *Adam: You invited the teachers to my house, where I sleep?!*
> *Bev: It's all because you told me to reach out to them.*
> *Adam: I said to leave them alone!*
> *Bev: Good thing I misheard you.*
> *Adam: Mom, there are certain things you just don't do: poop at school, hold hands with your sister, and invite teachers to a civilian residence!*

While this hilarious sitcom is parodying an extreme version of an overly involved parent, there will be some parents in real-life that will overstep the bounds. They are generally well-meaning and seeking connection. You can't fault them for that, but boundaries need to be maintained for structure, consistency, confidentiality, and equity.

HARD TO REACH

There will always be parents who are hard to reach or difficult to engage. Maybe they work two or more jobs or are struggling with health or family issues. In some families, fathers might be less involved because the mother is the designated school contact. (I was actually told once by a dad, "My wife handles all this stuff.") While we can't change family dynamics, we can make efforts to help parents feel more welcome in their child's school *stuff*.

I recall one child who was referred to the office frequently. I would email her parent and often get no response. I followed up with a phone call only to get one word responses in a dismissive manner. After a few attempts of reaching out, I invited the parent in for a meeting with the entire grade level team. It was time for everyone to connect and get on the same page on effective ways to support the child. The room was set up in a circle as an inviting arrangement to encourage discussion. We started the meeting by asking her to share some insights about her child. She talked almost the entire time. It was unbelievable. Obviously, email and phone calls were not the way to connect with this particular parent. She added a comment at the end that she is always available via text or phone calls. I could see the confused look on one of the teacher's faces who had never had her emails or calls returned. Regardless, actions speak louder than words. Now we knew the best way to connect with this particular parent was a face-to-face meeting.

If you're new to the school community, ask teachers and staff who have been there for a long time what they have done to engage families. If your experience is like mine, you may run into comments that are dismissive such as, "These parents don't care," or "You'll never get them to come to the school for that." If you hear this, try not to get discouraged. Keep asking until you find someone who is more optimistic about parent engagement efforts. In Dr. Jeff Prickett's book *Becoming Principal: A Leadership Journey & the Story of a School Community* (2021), he writes about his experience as an elementary principal in a community with a high percentage of Spanish-speaking households. He was fortunate to have an administrative assistant who was bilingual in Spanish and English who assisted him by posting signs in the community's native language. Dr. Prickett tells a story about how he partnered with a family to host a coffee chat in their home. The families responded favorably to this invitation because he met them on their turf.

This isn't quite a realistic model for a classroom teacher to follow, but it may be something teachers can suggest to their administration. Teachers can individually take smaller steps to increase parent engagement. If you know that a family speaks a language other than English at home and might not be comfortable reading emails in English, seek out someone on the staff who might be able to translate. Katja Frazier notes, in her 2015 article for "Edutopia,"

> Parents who do not speak English well may feel uncomfortable getting involved with their children's schools or have trouble communicating with school staff. However, school efforts to engage parents who do not speak English as their native language may improve their level of involvement.

Alternatively, the family might feel more comfortable reading and writing in English than speaking on the phone or in person. Ask more about the mode of communication they prefer, whether it is text or email. As a former expat living in a non-English speaking country, I know firsthand that it means a lot when the person who is trying to communicate with you makes an effort to improve their level of communication.

Beyond languages, some families may truly want to attend conferences, coffee talks, and parent nights, but their schedule may not allow it. Within the constraints of your school's open hours, try to offer some meeting times in the evening, early morning, during lunch, or on Zoom. Recording a meeting also increases accessibility. This may not be a realistic schedule for every event, but make some exceptions for parents who may need the flexibility.

On a personal note, I grew up in the '80s with a single mom. She worked a full-time job and attended community college classes in the evenings. Despite her busy schedule, she did her absolute best to make it to every school event. I remember a time that my first grade teacher, Mrs. Davis, brought me to her home after school and helped me get ready for the school play that evening. Even though I was only six years old, I remember being on stage dressed as Little Miss Muffett and seeing my mom in the audience. I didn't know at the time why Mrs. Davis brought me to her house, but now I know that she offered to help me get ready for the play because my mom had to work. Keep in mind this was the '80s and was acceptable back then. Now, it is highly ill-advised and possibly illegal for a teacher to drive a student anywhere. But the point still resonates today about a teacher who made the extra effort to help my family out in a time of need.

OVERLY NEEDY

There are some parent conversations that seem to be a cry for help from the parents. There are times I can't blame them. Sometimes, parent conferences start off with a team of the student's teachers sitting in a semicircle taking turns telling the parents all the mistakes and flaws that they see in their child. This cannot feel good to the parent and usually doesn't end well. If the parent doesn't get defensive or angry, then they might throw their hands up and basically say to the teacher, "Help! I don't know what else to do!"

Conversations with parents that turn into parent advice sessions make me uncomfortable. Not every educator in the room is a parent, nor has any expertise in parenting advice, even if they are parents. Furthermore, no educator knows the whole story of what the home dynamic is like – how do they interact with siblings? Who cares for the child while the parents work? What other family stressors might exist?

If a parent is seemingly in need of parenting advice, stick to school-related issues only. Explain the school expectations and how parents can be more aware of those expectations. "The upcoming test dates are posted on the class website a week in advance. Is there a way that you and your child can look at the test calendar together?" Being inquisitive over directive fosters a sense of ownership in the decision-making for the parents. I have used directives before with parents that were NOT helpful, such as, "Sit down together with your child with the class website, and add the test dates to your family planner." One, I do not know if the parent and child can realistically sit together to skim the class website. Plus, this sounds like a recipe for an argument if the student is a teenager. Two, I am assuming they have a family planner or shared calendar. This idealized family I am describing in this directive might only exist on Pinterest boards. If possible, be more coach-like when parents seem to be asking for parenting help. Being coach-like means staying curious, asking questions, and really listening to what they have to say. For more information on staying coach-like, check out Michael Bungay Stanier's book, *The Coaching Habit: Say Less, Ask More & Change the Way You Lead Forever* (2016).

As an educator with over 20 years of experience with teens, I feel quite comfortable reassuring parents that their child is going to be ok even if they get in trouble. As a middle school administrator, I made many calls to parents who had never heard a negative word about their child before my call. Some of these parents did not have older children so they were understandably nervous and concerned when their sweet, angelic child made a mistake. One parent asked me if this particular instance of their child's poor decision-making was a red flag. I realized at that point that this parent needed a lot of comforting around the fact that middle schoolers are going to make dumb mistakes, and in no way does this mean there is a red flag. I often explain to parents that adolescents have an underdeveloped prefrontal cortex, (AACAP, 2016), which means that they have difficulty predicting the consequences of their choices. This is one of the reasons we do not allow young teens to drive cars and sign contracts. Parents may not be aware of brain development, but once they learn a little bit about it, they can start to understand the bizarre choices their child makes. If their children are not teens yet, it helps to explain that young children are exploring boundaries and learning by pushing those boundaries and realizing the consequences.

There may be times that a parent's need for parenting advice goes beyond what a classroom teacher can offer. If the family or the child needs advice and support that exceeds academic or basic social guidance, it is better for a mental health care professional to step in. Teachers can offer suggestions and resources for families while also referring the family to the school's specialized faculty that fits their needs.

PARENTS FRUSTRATED WITH HOMEWORK HELP

Parents expressing frustration over homework is quite common, especially with math and languages, it seems. Perhaps this section should not be included in a chapter on extreme engagement because homework frustration is not an extreme parent complaint, but it is a frequent one. Helping your child with their homework can cause many fights at the kitchen table, especially as the child approaches their teen years. As a math teacher, I have heard many parents express feelings of embarrassment because they do not remember how to do the math their child is doing in class. Some parents also get quite emotional (and rightly so) when they see their child struggling to the point of tears when the homework is frustrating or confusing. Sometimes, homework is out of the reach of a student's capability to work independently. Naturally, parents want to jump in and help with a not helpful question, "Where are your notes on this?!" The notes may not be legible or complete, or they may not even exist. As you can tell, this interaction is headed for disaster. Homework can also interfere with family home life. Children lose sleep and/or miss meals because they are overwhelmed by too much work. A parent once emailed me a photo of their sleeping child explaining that she couldn't finish the homework I assigned. The photo was a bit over the top, but I got her point.

On the flip side, some parents demand rigorous homework. If a teacher does not regularly assign written homework assignments, these parents might complain to the administration. "How will my child get enough practice," they'll plead.

You might be reading this thinking, "Well, I am darned if I do and darned if I don't" when it comes to homework. The answer might lie in three words: meaningful, respectful, and personalized. This is what the Park School in Baltimore has determined for their family-friendly homework policy. In an article by Alison Baran titled "Evaluating the Role of Homework" in the Winter 2022 issue of NAIS Independent School Magazine, the Park School writes in their Homework Philosophy statement, "We believe in homework that is meaningful, purposeful, and designed to meet students' needs." If your school or your course adopted a similar homework policy, the kitchen table fights over homework might decline; therefore, making parents a little less frustrated with the teacher.

You might be reading this and possibly agree with such a homework policy, but you still need your students to practice concepts outside of class. The following example of a homework assignment comes from an upper elementary math class. (I chose math for the sample because of the frequent frustration math homework can conjure.)

Compare the following two homework assignments that provide practice on adding and subtracting decimals. How do the two examples of assignments demonstrate a practice that is meaningful, respectful, and personalized?

Traditional Assignment

20 problems adding and subtracting decimals
1) 2.13 + 34.12
2) 45.82 - 9.01
3) 12.34 + 10.10
....and so on for 20 problems.

Suggested Assignment

One problem
You are buying a book at the store for $4.15, a ball for $15.20, and a lollipop for $0.85. How much is your total purchase? Show your steps for finding your answer.
Try this: If you give the cashier a 20-dollar bill and a 5-dollar bill, will you get change back? How do you know? What bills can you give the cashier to pay for the purchase? List three possible answers.
Challenge: Write your own adding/subtracting decimals word problem and provide an answer key.

The traditional assignment is definitely solid practice of the concept – 20 times! And if you are a parent of a child struggling with the content, then it means banging your head against the wall – 20 times! If a student can do five of them is that enough to practice the concept? The suggested one-problem assignment certainly isn't one problem – but it seems like just one problem and might be perceived as less overwhelming. The initial problem provides basic practice and the *try this* and *challenge* follow up questions provide learners who are ready for an extension to dive deeper into the concept. The language of *try this* and *challenge* also suggests that going on to the additional problems is optional, which might be welcomed on a busy or stressful evening at home. After working out this one-problem, some students and their parents might even find the assignment, dare I say, fun?

The provided sample assignment serves as a model for how to make a repetitive assignment appear simultaneously shorter and more challenging. The parents who demand rigor will love the opportunity for extension and challenge. (They especially love it when you mention that their child was one of the few students who tackled the challenge problem!)

Additionally, you can scaffold homework assignments by providing a short video for the students and parents to watch that demonstrates the steps and directions. Because of the amount of time it takes to make a video, reserve this added feature for the homework assignments on a particularly complex assignment. To read more on the purpose of homework, check out the Vox article, "Nobody knows what the point of homework is" by Jacob Sweet (2023).

TEACHING COLLEAGUES' CHILDREN

This section is reserved for teachers who also have children at the same school or when you have issues teaching the children of your colleagues. Some schools directly address this with their employees. I worked at a school that held a special faculty meeting for employees with children at the same school. The Head of the School explicitly said, "If you see your child on campus during the day, do not hug them." I know he was well-intentioned, but EXCUSE

ME!? How do you explain to a preschooler that they can't hug mommy when they see her at school. Some schools will prohibit teachers from teaching their own children - this is not always possible in small schools. One student I know had his dad as his Arabic teacher and his mom as his science teacher. They were the only teachers for those subjects in his grade level. I have a personal connection to this section because I also taught at the same school as my child. I set boundaries for my family such as: you cannot ask me to sign a form or test during the day, you cannot hang out in my classroom when you are supposed to be somewhere else, and you cannot use my classroom as your personal locker (I will admit this last boundary was tested a lot). Other colleagues at the same school set different boundaries with their children. One teacher I knew would ask her child during the day what grade he earned on an assignment and within the same day, walk over to the teacher for an impromptu conference about it. That's where colleagues can cross a line with each other.

Educators are professionals who deserve the respect of an appointment request, even from colleagues. If you are a parent who has initiated a conference on the fly with your child's teacher, I ask you to reconsider this practice. Yes, you might be friends, and it may not seem to bother the teacher. And yes, you might really need to share some information about your child with their teacher. Instead, consider sending an email to ask for a good time to meet with the teacher. As a friend/colleague you will probably get priority VIP access to the teacher, and that is to be expected. At least, you took the courteous approach by asking for an appointment first.

Sometimes, you might find yourself in the awkward position of teaching a student whose parent is a boundary-breaking colleague. This can be a tough situation because you want to look out for your colleague, especially if they are a friend as well. The best advice is to be direct but delicate. If a colleague is coming in unannounced to discuss their child in your class, you can ask them for more time to prepare documentation and data. Try this: "I'd love to chat with you about April's recent essay, but I need to look more closely at the rubric so that I am better prepared to talk with you. There were parts of the rubric that she needed some improvement on, and right now, I can't remember what they were off the top of my head. Can we meet tomorrow after lunch?" With a response like this, you are acknowledging that you see a need for improvement in their child's work, but at the same time, you are asking for the time to be prepared to speak about it in an informed manner. Hopefully, after one or maybe even two times hearing a response like this, they will realize that you need a preset appointment before discussing their child's progress.

To be honest, the relationship with the colleague will last longer than the relationship of being the teacher for their child. The child will leave your class after a year (in most cases), but you will still work with their parent as a coworker and maybe as a friend. If you are too direct or hard-nosed about limiting interactions, it could damage the collegial relationship. If the child is having major academic or discipline issues, go to the parent first out of courtesy. Explain to your colleague that you have to talk with the appropriate administration, but you wanted them to know first. There are definite perks to working at the same school as your child, but it's important not to abuse the privilege with your teacher colleagues.

REFLECTION

- Think back on how your own parents engaged with your school? Were they involved with volunteering? What motivated their involvement or lack thereof?

- How can you manage expectations with parents who are too helpful? Do they need guidelines or restrictions that help them maintain a healthy level of involvement?

- Consider your school community. Are school events well attended? Is it the same small group of parents who attend most events? What can be adjusted to welcome more parents into the school? How can you reach out beyond the school building?

- What do you say to parents who seek parenting help?

- Are there ways to adjust your class's assigned homework to be more respectful, purposeful, and personalized?

- What are the perks and challenges you've experienced teaching colleagues' children?

Chapter 9
Parent–teacher conferences and parent night

Parent Night. Open House. Meet the Teacher. Whatever the name is, it might be the first time a teacher faces an audience of parents. I do not intend to add to the already existing pressure of such an event, but it can be somewhat of a make-or-break moment for a teacher. I am sure that there is plenty of evidence to contradict that statement. I have known teachers who missed the event because of an illness or other unavoidable circumstances who, nonetheless, have had a successful year building great relationships with parents. Teachers who are new to the school face even more pressure for this event. The parents want to know: What is the teacher like? Are they nice? Do they seem competent?

I prefer parent night to be scheduled a few weeks into the school year. You know the students a little, and they know you a little. The students have already set the stage for the first impression from the parents' perspective. By the time you meet with the parents, they have, hopefully, started to develop a positive impression of you because of their child's stories about school. And you can share little tidbits like, "This class is quite inquisitive, I love how often they ask questions about science!"

Stories from the Field

Denise of Houston, MN (currently Platteville, WI)
Last conference of the night, finished talking about their delightful daughter, ended up talking about the music we loved. Next time I saw them, they brought me a Neil Young mixtape (yes, it was the early 90s) to keep.

Teacher, Bill Velto, writes in a "Teacher Going Gradeless" blog post "How I Learned to Stop Worrying and Love Parent-Teacher Conferences" (n.d.),

> ...the approaching date of parent-teacher conferences filled me with dread. And I know I wasn't the only one. Talking with colleagues, we would psych

ourselves up and tell each other that we were fine. We really meant F.I.N.E. (Freaked Out, Insecure, Neurotic, and Emotional), as in the acronym from the 2003 movie *The Italian Job,* but whatever.

MAKING PARENT NIGHT MEANINGFUL FOR PARENTS

Depending on the size of your school, parents may be invited on campus during the day for parent conferences or maybe to a Parent Night. Small schools tend to open their doors more often for parent presentations from teachers such as literacy night, math night, parent coffees, etc. Teachers have a long list of preparation items for Parent Night such as decorating the room just so, sharing samples of student work, pronouncing the parents' names correctly, and most important of all, not looking incompetent in front of the parents. Just as important is making the night meaningful and informative for families, avoiding the fluff.

Drs. Robert Evans and Michael Thompson suggest, in their 2021 book, *Hopes and Fears: Working with Today's Independent School Par-*

ents, that teachers address parents' fears and worries during their presentation. Teachers can help parents predict what's to come in the new grade level. As an example, "You may have heard that there is a significant increase in homework from third to fourth grade. (Pause for head nodding and affirmative murmuring.) I can assure you that we guide our incoming fourth graders by teaching them organizational skills that will help them manage their workload. We also offer homework help time after school for students who have additional questions." In this example, you're not denying that the workload increases, but you're assuaging parents' worries about whether their child can handle it. Don't shy away from the real stuff parents want to hear.

GRACEFULLY AVOID INDIVIDUAL FEEDBACK CONVERSATIONS

Most likely, a parent or two will approach you directly during Parent Night to ask about their individual child's progress so far (even if Parent Night is only two weeks into the school year). This has happened to me every single year I have been in the classroom. Every. Single. Year.

I thought it was polite to answer their questions about their child's progress. A line of waiting parents would form, so I would rush my answer to try to get to everyone before they had to visit the next teacher. This wasn't fair to the parents, nor to me. Now, I politely tell parents who are seeking individual feedback that I would be happy to talk with them in detail at another time. "It is great to have Olivia in my class this year. Regarding her progress so far, would you mind sending me an email? We can continue this conversation when I can dedicate more time." A response like this confirms that you do know who their child is, that you like them, and that you respect them so much that you want to dedicate time to talk in detail. Most of the time the parents do not follow up with an email. They are probably satisfied with meeting you and knowing that you know their child.

BETTER PARENT–TEACHER CONFERENCES

Sitting down one-on-one with parents is very different from presenting at Parent Night. The focus is shifting away from you, as the teacher, and solely on the student being discussed. The conference has shifted to a two-way dialogue rather than a one-way delivery of information. Parents want to get to know you as their child's teacher (How Two-Way Communication Can Boost Parent Engagement, 2018).

They also want to feel at ease that their child is in the care of an educator who genuinely cares about them. This care is communicated through relationship building and kind honesty about their child's progress. When a parent comes in to meet with the teacher it is important to note that the parent can be nervous. They might be apprehensive about how their child is performing in school compared to the other students. Kind honesty means sharing objective observations about their child while also recognizing their child's strengths. "Evelyn has a natural tendency toward leadership. This leadership shows up in her group work with classmates. She also recently led a group of her friends to run down the hall. She was asked to write a reflection on the safety concerns of running in the school hallways. We want to foster her leadership skills while also helping her make decisions that keep the community safe. How do you see Evelyn's leadership emerging at home?" This conversation starter tells the parent you see their child – the good and the not so good. It also reveals an objectively observed behavior and the subsequent consequence for that behavior. The teacher is communicating that the school is working WITH the parent and child to promote prosocial behavior. The teacher then ends with a question that invites the parent to share insight about their child from a home perspective.

There are times that no matter how much the teacher tries to foster a two-way discussion, they are just not getting much traction with the parent. When a parent comes in for a meeting and there is not much to report because the student is meeting expectations, it can be difficult to think of things to say. In these situations, I lean on a common piece of advice that may help in uncertain parent conferences: "If you don't know what to do, do what you know." What we do know well as educators is how to listen. Let the parent(s) talk first. Really listen to what they value and what they fear. Respond to their comments with empathy and suggestions as you see appropriate. If listening isn't a strength of yours, check out Celeste Headlee's Ted Talk *10 ways to have a better conversation* (2012). Her tenth tip focuses on listening specifically.

> Why do we not listen to each other? Number one, we'd rather talk. When I'm talking, I'm in control. I don't have to hear anything I'm not interested in. I'm the center of attention. I can bolster my own identity. But there's another reason: We get distracted... And look, I know, it takes effort and energy to actually pay attention to someone, but if you can't do that, you're not in a conversation. You're just two people shouting out barely re-lated sentences in the same place.

By deeply listening to the parent, you might find that a student who appears to be meeting all the expectations at school has more issues to address than you previously knew.

Another pro tip, suggested by Elli Carroll in a 2021 Edutopia article "4 Ways to Make Parent-Teacher Conferences Easier," is to provide stu-dent work for the parents to view. Carroll writes,

Providing authentic work at conferences shows the following: 1. You *do* grade work. 2. Whether a parent's perception of their child's level of effort matches what the student is *really* doing. Many teachers find success having students choose a writing piece in their notebook to bookmark or another assignment or test that they are proud of. This always puts a smile on parents' faces, the kids get to show off a bit, and you don't have to go looking for something. It's a win-win-win!

If artifacts of student work aren't applicable or available, ask each student to complete a semester reflection sheet that you can share with parents. This is a sample used for sixth grade math students at the end of the grading period. This can be adjusted for younger or older students as needed. The students completed it in class knowing that we would be sharing the sheet with their parents at the upcoming conferences.

Form created by Crystal Frommert
Printable version can be found at www.crystalfrommert.com

UNSCHEDULED CONFERENCES

In the schools where I have taught, there was a designated day or two for parent conferences (either just parents or students and parents together). Of course, there will be other times outside of these two designated dates that you will need to meet with parents face to face. Some of these meetings may be initiated by the teacher because there is a concern about progress or behavior that cannot wait until the next conference day. Parents may request a conference with you over a concern they have regarding their child. This request can be anxiety-producing for many teachers if they do not

146

know the reason for the conference. It may help to ask, "May I know the nature of our meeting so that I can prepare before we meet?"

There are also a few conferences that will straight up annoy the teacher. Once a parent emailed me the day after our school's designated conference day to inform me that they were in the Cayman Islands and would need to schedule a meeting when they returned. (This was before Zoom was a popular alternative.) The expectation at my school, and probably at yours too, is that we make the time to meet with parents when they request it (even if they chose to take a Caribbean vacation during our conference days.) Perhaps the most annoying conference of all is the "pop-in." Hopefully, your school's front desk has a security check-in where parents must obtain a pass before entering the building. But if a parent dishonestly tells the receptionist that they have an appointment with a teacher, they might be allowed in without verification of a meeting. Ideally, the pop in is well-intentioned, and you can politely ask the parent to schedule a time to come back; alternatively, they just had a quick question that they assumed you could answer in a few minutes. The annoying part is the timing. Parents can pop in at the beginning of the day when you're setting up the classroom or at the end of the day when you're planning or wrapping up. It can even happen mid-day during your planning period when you're grading or planning. The worst of these is the angry pop-in. These are rare but are the hardest to deflect. Ideally, you can walk the parent down to the administration offices to get backup. If this isn't possible, slyly text a neighboring teacher to come rescue you with a fake faculty meeting reminder. Remember that parents owe you the respect of requesting a meeting ahead of time, and you owe them the respect of honoring their request.

REFLECTION

- What languages are predominantly spoken in your school community? Do you have staff/faculty who can translate parent letters and conferences for parents who do not speak the same language as the teacher?

- Are the parents in your community used to communicating via text, phone, in person, letter, or email? How can you differentiate your communication modes to reach your parents effectively?

- Does your school have a security check-in to prevent visitors from popping in unannounced? Have you and your neighboring colleagues set up a text code to indicate that a rescue is needed?

- How are you actively helping all families feel welcome? Are all families contacted with equal frequency for both positive and negative reasons?

Chapter 10

Report card comments and narratives

Every school I've ever worked at has varying expectations around report card comments. One school didn't require any. One school accepted and even promoted boilerplate copy and pasting. One school required a personalized, unique narrative for every student. One middle/high school wanted comments directed to the student such as "Boris, you had a strong Term 2 in Biology…"

I am not sure that any of these comment expectations is necessarily the right way to do it; it depends on the school's culture. In order to meet your school's expectations around comments, ask a veteran teacher to show you some samples of their previous years' comments. Here are a few tips I have picked up along the way throughout my comment-writing career.

- <u>Start with the student's name.</u> A parent once confided in me that he didn't start reading the comment until he saw his kid's name. The general introduction sentence about the course or the curriculum is not interesting to him. To hook readers like him, I started writing introductory sentences like this, "Emerson is enjoying our current unit on operations with fractions..." Gotcha! You just read the general curriculum summary sentence! After you summarize the units of study, mention how the student is approaching and progressing with the unit. "She seemed to enjoy our fractions bingo game, especially multiplying and dividing fractions. Emerson is encouraged to attend some tutorial sessions to get more practice with adding and subtracting fractions."

- **To save time, write five template comments** ranging from struggling students to excelling students. As you go down the list of your class, choose one of the five categories for each student. Copy and paste the template but change a few phrases to personalize the comment to that individual student's progress. This is not cheating or being lazy - this is simply a jumping-off point that saves time rather than starting every comment from scratch. Be sure to change names and pronouns as well if you copy and paste from a template.

- Speaking of pronouns, if a student identifies by a different name or pronoun in class than what is officially stated on school records, approach your comment writing carefully, especially if the parents are unaware of or disagree with the student's preferences. This is for the safety of the student. Consult with administration and the counseling team on what identifiers to use in report card comments. This is a controversial take, but some schools recommend avoiding pronouns altogether on official report cards if there is a discrepancy between what the parents and student use as the student's pronouns. In person, use the name and pronouns with which the student identifies.

- Forget the compliment sandwich model. The critique can get lost in the middle of the sandwich. Instead, start with a student's strength, followed by feedback on improvement needed, ending with an action item on how to improve. "Rocky is working hard on operations with fractions this term. In fact, he demonstrated a multiplication problem on the board for the entire class. He is having difficulty determining the operation needed in word problems. He and I talked about a strategy to help with this. If he temporarily substitutes the fractions in the word problem with whole numbers, the operation needed becomes clearer. We will continue practicing this in the next term as well."

– <u>Avoid too much fluff.</u> Be specific and to the point. Aim for a tone that expresses hope, care, and honesty. As of this writing, using ChatGPT to write comments seems to produce fluffy and generic comments that are not personal to the student or the class.

HOW WE MIGHT BE PENALIZING THE QUIET STUDENTS

While this book can't address every type of student characteristic that might be addressed in a report card comment, I do want to highlight the recurring feedback that introverted students receive. As mentioned in the "Learning for Justice" article titled "Quiet in the Classroom" (2014),

> Consider this report card comment. It is very common. If you are a teacher, perhaps you've written it yourself: 'He's a great student, but he's quiet in class. I wish he'd speak up more often. When he speaks up, he has a lot to offer.' Now imagine if this comment were written about some other aspect of a student's identity. I doubt it would be received as well. In fact, it might even cause an uproar.

This was a report card comment that I wrote about my quiet students regularly. After reading Susan Cain's book, *Quiet: The Power of Introverts in a World That Can't Stop Talking* (2013), I shifted the way I wrote about my less talkative students. I would often get feedback from parents like, "Yes, I know she is quiet in class - teachers have been saying this for years." Why do we think we need to turn our introverted students into extroverts? Are there other ways to get them engaged in class that do not require an identity change? David Cutler writes about how to dig deeper to find the strengths of our more quiet students in his 2016 "Edutopia article," "Quiet: Susan Cain on Approaching Introverted Students."

> I think it is a matter of finding one-on-one time with those students, figuring out what are the areas that they're really interested in, and maybe calling on them or asking them to participate around those areas. Giving them extra assignments around their areas of passion.

What about the value of class participation? In an article Jessica Lahey posted originating in 2015 on QuietRev.com and later updated for the Huffington Post (2017), she argues that class participation is valuable to assess in her class. She and a parent disagreed about how this portion of the student's grade is biased against introverted students. Lahey's take on class participation grades evolved as she read more about introverted and shy students. She suggests the following ideas,

The teacher poses a question to the class and asks students to first reflect on or write down their answer and then share it with a peer. Sometimes, a shy student can find confidence through the encouragement of a single peer before sharing his idea with the larger classroom. I learned that while it can be inconvenient to accommodate different personality types, it's worth it.

I took Cain's advice to heart, particularly: "Both parents and teachers can work with a child one-on-one, offering strategies for participation—such as offering a comment early in class, before anticipatory anxiety grows too strong." I made a specific effort to employ this practice with the mother and student I'd been struggling to understand, and it improved our relationship overnight.

REFLECTION

- Do you remember any comments from your own report cards as a child? (A common comment on my report cards was "talks too much in class.")

- If you teach older students, are you writing for your student or their parents as the audience?

- In what ways can you streamline comment writing but also make them meaningful and personalized?

- Do you find yourself writing comments that suggest a student changes a part of their identity, such as introverted behavior or talking loudly?

Conclusion

There's no doubt that no matter how much effort you put into effective communication with parents, there will inevitably be bumps in the road. The best an educator can do is set the tone for the relationship early, keep parents updated, and not take it personally when there is tension in the relationship. A parent wrote to me after a school trip, "Thank you for taking care of our precious treasures." She was exactly right. Our students are their parents' treasures. Hopefully, educators' and parents' goals are aligned in efforts to educate the child. Effective teacher-parent communication can help to keep these goals aligned. When parents feel that their child's teacher cares for their child, then it is much easier to get on the same page.

Renee DuChainey-Farkes summed this up beautifully in her interview with the Enrollment Spectrum Podcast (Baron & Mundahl, 2022). In this interview it can be initially off-putting to hear that partnering with parents (regardless of tuition-based or public education) is a "customer experience." The term customer experience is used to describe the parent/teacher relationship similar to that of a "customer of a business" relationship. Relationships between schools and parents are far more profound and meaningful than that. She further comments on the parent partnership by reminding educators that parents are craving relationships. Teachers see their children day after day in a very different setting than at home. We hear what their kids say and see what lights them up. Sometimes, kids do not fully show this side of themselves in the home setting. Parents desperately want to know what we know about their kid – their precious child.

After reading the preceding chapters on communication with parents, consider the following key points:

1. Reach out early

2. Have the hard conversations

3. Differentiate communication

REACH OUT EARLY

The start of the school year is a hectic time for educators, and it is easy to leave parent communication by the wayside. Carve out the time to reach out to each family individually. It will be worth it. If you have your class roster before school starts, send an email to each family welcoming them to the class. Some educators make home visits before school starts. (Check with your school's administration before deciding to visit your students' homes.) If you teach multiple classes with many students, break up the task and send a few emails a day during the first couple of weeks of school. Try to include a short anecdote about the child, "Tarek volunteers an answer everyday for the Daily Grammar Practice." If you suspect a student will need special parent communication earlier than most of the students (for behavior, academics, etc.), reach out to these families first. You want the first contact to be a positive one. End the first contact with an action item – "Hope to see you at Open House on September 15 at 6pm." Starting off the year with personal and positive connections serves many purposes. It shows parents that you are approachable, you are enthusiastic about working with their child, and you see their child as an individual with special talents and gifts.

HAVE THE HARD CONVERSATIONS

Another key point is to face the hard conversations when needed. Most likely, such conversations should be conducted on the phone or in-person, no matter how uncomfortable that can be. As educators, we are responsible for telling parents our concerns about their child's progress and offering possible solutions. When approaching an uncomfortable conversation, use language that encourages a partnership with the parent. We are on the same side. Hard conversations are even harder when, as the teacher, we must admit to making a mistake. This happens to all of us. The best we can do is work to make it right. Furthermore, some hard conversations do not involve any misstep on the part of the teacher, but the parent still takes that perspective. Avoid becoming defensive, instead remain professional by standing in confidence of your experience and expertise. Seek assistance from a school administrator if you anticipate a hard conversation might get out of control. You have the right to end any meeting if you feel uncomfortable.

DIFFERENTIATE COMMUNICATION

The last key point from the book is to personalize communication. Parents are like snowflakes – no one parent is identical to another. Some parents need more hand holding and reassurance regarding their child's progress. Some parents are only reachable by text, some prefer a phone call or in-person meeting. Some parents pore over your class newsletter the minute it is published, some parents have no idea that grades are available online. There is a broad range of parent communication levels. As you get to know what each family needs and prefers, you can more effectively communicate, which will foster more solid partnerships. This does not mean that you need to give out your personal number or text parents late into the night. By setting and honoring healthy boundaries for yourself, you can avoid burnout and resentment.

Parent communication is never perfect so don't aim for any resemblance of perfection. You will mess up, parents will mess up, kids will mess up. It's inevitable. Have compassion for yourself and others through this journey. Each time there is a failure of effective communication, try to view it as a learning opportunity. Ask yourself, "Ok, that didn't work, what can I learn from this for next time?" Each time you interact with a parent, you are building the foundation for success for the student. While working with parents won't always be smooth sailing, as educators, we must keep trying to build strong partnerships to give the student the support they deserve.

Acknowledgements

I would like to take this opportunity to express my heartfelt gratitude to the individuals and organizations who have supported and contributed to the completion of this project.

Special thank you to Darrin Peppard for your encouragement and coaching throughout this journey. I would also like to express my appreciation to Jessica Peppard for being such a detailed and smart editor. Your keen eye and expert feedback have helped to shape this work into its final form.

Thank you to Edutopia, Marva Hinton, and Tom Berger for giving me the opportunity to grow as a writer. Your platform has provided a space for me to share my ideas and connect with a wider community of educators.

Thank you to my sister Mandy Gagliardi whose talents and honesty help me to be a better writer.

I am also grateful to Greg Frommert for creating this eye-catching book cover. Your creativity and talent are beyond impressive.

Thank you to the inspiring administrators and colleagues who have taught me so much over the years. Your support and encouragement have helped me to grow both personally and professionally.

I would also like to extend my appreciation to the supportive parents of my students for partnering with me to help our kids grow and learn.

My gratitude goes out to Heather Cherry, Brian Martin, Steve Barkley, Dr. John Golden, Dr. Rob Evans, and Dr. Michael Thompson for writing endorsements of my work. Your kind words and support mean the world to me.

Finally, a heartfelt thank you to all the teachers out there who work tirelessly to educate and inspire our children. Your dedication and passion for your craft are truly admirable.

References

Aacap. (n.d.). Teen brain: Behavior, problem solving, and decision making. Retrieved March 22, 2022, from https://www.aacap.org/aacap/families_and_youth/facts_for_families/fff-guide/the-teen-brain-behavior-problem-solving-and-decision-making-095.aspx

Aguilar, E. (2016, October 11). *5 ways to create a strong parent partnership*. Edutopia. Retrieved March 22, 2022, from https://www.edutopia.org/article/5-ways-create-strong-parent-partnership-elena-aguilar

An, S. (2019, August 15). *Changing classrooms: When students are black and teachers are white*. NPR. Retrieved March 22, 2022, from https://www.npr.org/local/309/2019/08/15/751199037/changing-classrooms-when-students-are-black-and-teachers-are-white

Anderson, M. D. (2016, November 15). *Stereotypes are at the heart of parent-teacher communication*. The Atlantic. Retrieved March 22, 2022, from https://www.theat-

lantic.com/education/archive/2016/11/
which-parents-are-teachers-most-likely-
to-contact/507755/

*Anti-bias policies that really work in Customer
Service*. Harvard Business Review. (2021,
November 2). Retrieved March 22, 2022,
from https://hbr.org/podcast/2021/11/
anti-bias-policies-that-really-work-in-cus-
tomer-service

Bannister, N. (2022, March 22). *"Tell me more
about my child's learning" - new research
reveals parents hungry for more person-
alised information from schools*. FE
News. Retrieved March 18, 2023, from
https://www.fenews.co.uk/education/
tell-me-more-about-my-childs-learning-
new-research-reveals-parents-hungry-
for-more-personalised-information-from-
schools/

Bender, Y. (2005). *The tactful teacher: Effective
communication with parents, colleagues,
and administrators*. Nomad Press.

Burden, P. R. (2012). *Classroom management:
Creating a successful K-12 Learning
Community*. Wiley.

Cain, S. (2013). *Quiet: The power of introverts in a world that can't stop talking*. Broadway Paperbacks.

Carroll, E. (2021, November 12). *4 ways to make parent-teacher conferences easier*. Edutopia. Retrieved March 22, 2022, from https://www.edutopia.org/article/4-ways-make-parent-teacher-conferences-easier

Cassetta, G. (2013). *No more taking away recess and other problematic discipline practices*. Heinemann.

Craft, J., & Callahan, J. (2019). *New kid*. Harper, an imprint of HarperCollinsPublishers.

Cutler, D. (2016, April 8). *Quiet: Susan Cain on approaching introverted students*. Edutopia. Retrieved March 22, 2022, from https://www.edutopia.org/discussion/quiet-susan-cain-approaching-introverted-students

Davidson. (2021). The Goldbergs. episode.

Dhawan, E. (2021). *Digital body language: How to build trust and connection, no matter the distance* (1st ed.). St. Martin's Press.

Erman Misirlisoy, P. D. (2021, July 20). *The 5:1 rule for better relationships*. Thrive Global. Retrieved March 22, 2022, from https://thriveglobal.com/stories/the-51-rule-for-better-relationships/

Evaluating the role of homework. NAIS. (n.d.). Retrieved March 22, 2022, from https://www.nais.org/magazine/independent-school/winter-2022/evaluating-the-role-of-homework/

Five do's and don'ts of effective parent communication: Independent School Management: Advancing school leadership-enriching the student experience. Independent School Management | Advancing School Leadership-Enriching The Student Experience. (2019, November 14). Retrieved March 22, 2022, from https://isminc.com/advisory/publications/the-source/five-dos-and-donts-effective-parent-communication

Frazier, K. (2015, October 20). *7 helpful tips for conferences with parents who speak minimal English*. Edutopia. Retrieved March 22, 2022, from https://www.edutopia.org/discussion/7-helpful-tips-conferences-parents-who-speak-minimal-english

Frommert, C. (2020, July 21). *A strategy for building productive relationships with parents*. Edutopia. Retrieved March 22, 2022, from https://www.edutopia.org/article/strategy-building-productive-relationships-parents

Gleeson, S. (2021, November 10). *Portugal made a law that bans texting employees after work. why? for more teleworkers*. USA Today. Retrieved March 22, 2022, from https://www.usatoday.com/story/news/world/2021/11/10/portugal-law-bans-boss-contact-employees-after-work-hours/6367092001/

Golstein, M. (2013). *Phoning parents high-leverage moves to Transform your classroom & restore your sanity*. match Education.

Hanawalt, Z. (2020, September 11). *Viral instagram post urges everyone to stop saying 'moms and Dads' in favor of 'grownups' when referring to kids' caregivers*. Parents. Retrieved March 22, 2022, from https://www.parents.com/parenting/better-parenting/viral-instagram-post-suggests-we-talk-about-kids-grown-ups-in-

stead-of-moms-and-dads-for-those-who-
don-t-have-traditional-families/

Headlee, C. (n.d.). *10 ways to have a better conversation*. Celeste Headlee: 10 ways to
have a better conversation | TED Talk.
Retrieved March 22, 2022, from https://
www.ted.com/talks/celeste_-
headlee_10_ways_to_have_a_better_-
conversation?language=en

*How to respond if a parent accuses you of
teaching sel or critical race theory*. Truth
For Teachers. (2022, September 13). Retrieved March 18, 2023, from https://
truthforteachers.com/truth-for-teachers-
podcast/teaching-critical-race-theory-
how-to-respond/

*How Two-way communication can boost parent
engagement*. Waterford.org. (2021, October 7). Retrieved March 22, 2022, from
https://www.waterford.org/education/
two-way-communication-parent-en-
gagement/

Keane, J. (2021, June 22). *The legal right to dis-
connect could become the norm in Eu-
rope*. CNBC. Retrieved March 22, 2022,
from https://www.cnbc.com/

2021/06/22/right-to-disconnect-could-
    become-the-norm-in-europe.html

Minero, E. (2018, October 5). *5 strategies for a
    successful parent-teacher conference*.
    Edutopia. Retrieved March 22, 2022,
    from https://www.edutopia.org/article/5-
    strategies-successful-parent-teacher-
    conference

Mundahl, P. B. and H., About the Author
    Peter Baron is EMA's chief member rela-
    tions officer, Peter Baron is EMA's chief
    member relations officer, & More Con-
    tent by Peter Baron and Hans Mundahl.
    (2022, October 13). *Are you thinking of
    your parents as partners? [EP.110]*. Learn-
    ing Center. Retrieved January 2, 2023,
    from https://learn.enrollment.org/en-
    rollment-spectrum-podcast/are-you-
    thinking-of-your-parents-as-partners-ep-
    110

NPR. (2022, May 4). *School colors episode 1:
    'there is no plan'*. NPR. Retrieved March
    18, 2023, from https://www.npr.org/tran-
    scripts/1096469394

Prickett, D. J. (2021). *Becoming principal: A leadership journey & the story of school community*. Road to Awesome, LLC.

Quiet in the classroom. Learning for Justice. (n.d.). Retrieved March 22, 2022, from https://www.learningforjustice.org/magazine/quiet-in-the-classroom

Ray, R., & Gibbons, A. (2022, March 9). *Why are states banning critical race theory?* Brookings. Retrieved March 22, 2022, from https://www.brookings.edu/blog/fixgov/2021/07/02/why-are-states-banning-critical-race-theory/

Reardon, K. K., Knight, R., & Whitehurst, J. (2021, September 1). *How to have difficult conversations when you don't like conflict*. Harvard Business Review. Retrieved March 22, 2022, from https://hbr.org/2017/05/how-to-have-difficult-conversations-when-you-dont-like-conflict

Revolution, Q. (2017, December 7). *I argued that class participation was necessary. then I heard from introverts*. HuffPost. Retrieved March 22, 2022, from https://www.huffpost.com/entry/class-participation-for-kids_n_7699926

Robson, D. (2022, February 25). *The digital body language cues you send – or don't send*. BBC Worklife. Retrieved March 22, 2022, from https://www.bbc.com/worklife/article/20210617-the-digital-body-language-cues-you-send-or-dont-send

The rude, demanding parents who bully schools. Dallas News. (2019, August 27). Retrieved March 22, 2022, from https://www.dallasnews.com/opinion/commentary/2016/06/17/the-rude-demanding-parents-who-bully-schools/

says:, E. P. (2022, March 1). *How to differentiate parent communication*. Truth For Teachers. Retrieved March 22, 2022, from https://thecornerstoneforteachers.com/truth-for-teachers-podcast/how-to-differentiate-parent-communication-set-healthy-boundaries/

School Library Journal. (n.d.). Retrieved March 22, 2022, from https://www.slj.com/?detailStory=jerry-craft-on-being-the-new-kid

Shakespeare, W. (1597). Romeo & Juliet.

Stanier, M. B. (2016). *The coaching habit: Say less, ask more & change the way you lead forever.* Page Two Books, Inc.

Strauss, L. (2020, January 16). *I'm a white teacher with a classroom of minority students. here's how I teach across race.* USA Today. Retrieved March 22, 2022, from https://www.usatoday.com/story/opinion/voices/2020/01/16/teaching-shortage-education-race-minority-column/4419331002/

Sweet, J. (2023, February 13). *Nobody knows what the point of homework is.* Vox. Retrieved March 18, 2023, from https://www.vox.com/the-highlight/23584497/remote-school-homework-elimination-movement

Thompson, M., & Evans, R. (2021). *Hopes and Fears: Working with Today's Independent School Parents.* NAIS.

Velto, B. (2022, December 4). *How I learned to stop worrying and love parent-teacher conferences.* Teachers Going Gradeless. Retrieved March 18, 2023, from https://www.teachersgoinggradeless.com/blog/pt-conferences

Why no one reads your classroom newsletter. Laura Candler. (2018, August 6). Retrieved March 22, 2022, from https://lauracandler.com/why-no-one-reads-your-newsletter/

About the Author

Crystal Frommert, M.Ed., has over 20 years of experience as an educator in public, parochial, and international schools. Beyond teaching middle and high school, she has served as an instructional coach, school board member, adjunct college instructor, technology coordinator, and administrator. She currently teaches middle school math in Houston, where she lives with her husband, daughter, and fluffy dog. Learn more about Crystal at www.crystalfrommert.com

More Books from Road to Awesome

Taking the Leap: A Field Guide for Aspiring
School Leaders by Robert F. Breyer

Transform: Techy Notes to Make Learning Sticky
by Debbie Tannenbaum

Becoming Principal: A Leadership Journey &
The Story of School Community by Dr. Jeff
Prickett

Elevate Your Vibe: Action Planning with Purpose
by Lisa Toebben

#OwnYourEpic: Leadership Lessons in Owning
Your Voice and Your Story by Dr. Jay Dostal

The Design Thinking, Entrepreneurial, Visionary
Planning Leader: A Practical guide for Thriving
in Ambiguity
by Dr. Michael Nagler

Becoming the Change: Five Essential Elements
to Being Your Best Self by Dan Wolfe

inspired: moments that matter
by Melissa Wright

Foundations of Instructional Coaching: Impact
People, Improve Instruction, Increase Success
by Ashley Hubner

Out of the Trenches: Stories of Resilient
Educators
by Dana Goodier

Principled Leader
by Bobby Pollicino

Road to Awesome: The Journey of a Leader
by Darrin Peppard

Children's Books from Road to Awesome

Road to Awesome A Journey for Kids
by Jillian DuBois and Darrin M. Peppard

Emersyn Blake and the Spotted Salamander
by Kim Collazo

Theodore Edward Makes a New Friend
by Alyssa Schmidt

Made in the USA
Las Vegas, NV
28 November 2023

81736073R00108